# BEAUTIFUL BIRDS

# LECTOR HOUSE PUBLIC DOMAIN WORKS

# BEAUTIFUL BIRDS

## EDMUND SELOUS

ISBN: 978-93-90314-06-5

Published:                    1901

**LECTOR HOUSE LLP**
E-MAIL: lectorpublishing@gmail.com

LYRE-BIRD

# BEAUTIFUL BIRDS

BY

## EDMUND SELOUS
AUTHOR OF "TOMMY SMITH'S ANIMALS"


## WITH MANY ILLUSTRATIONS BY
## HUBERT D. ASTLEY

1901

# CONTENTS

# LIST OF ILLUSTRATIONS

# BEAUTIFUL BIRDS

# CHAPTER I

## WHY BEAUTIFUL BIRDS ARE KILLED

What beautiful things birds are! Can you think of any other creatures that are quite so beautiful? I know you will say "Butterflies," and perhaps it *is* a race between the birds and the butterflies, but I think the birds win it even here in England. Just think of the Kingfisher, that bird that is like a little live chip of the blue sky, flying about all by itself, and doing just what it likes. The Sky-blue Butterfly is like that too, I know, but then it is a much smaller chip, and does not shine in the sun in such a wonderful way as the Kingfisher does. Neither, I think, does the Peacock-Butterfly, or the Red Admiral, or the Painted Lady, or the Greater or Lesser Tortoise-shell; and, besides, they none of them go so fast. Yes, all those butterflies are beautiful, very, very beautiful. But now, supposing they were all flying about in a field that a river was winding through, and, supposing you were sitting there too, amongst the daisies and buttercups in the bright summer sunshine, and looking at them, and supposing all at once there was a little dancing dot of light far away down the river, and that it came gleaming and gleaming along, getting nearer and nearer and keeping just in the middle all the time, till it passed you like a sapphire sunbeam, like a star upon a bird's wings, then I am sure you would look and look at it all the time it was coming, and look and look after it all the time it was going away, and when at last it was quite gone you would sit wondering, forgetting about the butterflies, and thinking only of that star-bird, that little jewelly gem. But, perhaps, if you were to see a *Purple Emperor* sweeping along—ah, *he* is a *very* magnificent butterfly, is the purple emperor. You can tell that from his name, but whether he is *quite* so magnificent as a star-bird (for that is what we will call the Kingfisher)—well, it is not so easy to decide. The birds and the butterflies are both beautiful, there is no doubt about that, only this little book is about beautiful birds, and perhaps afterwards there will be another one about beautiful butterflies. That will be quite fair to both.

The birds, then! We will talk about them. I am going to tell you about some of the most beautiful ones that there are, and to describe them to you, so that you will know something about what they are like. But perhaps you think that you know that already because you have seen them, so that *you* could tell *me* what they are like. There is the star-bird that we have been talking about, and then there is the Thrush and the Blackbird. What two more beautiful birds could you see than they, as they hop about over the lawn of your garden in the early dewy morning? The Blackbird is all over of such a dark, glossy, velvety black, and his bill is such a lovely, deep, orangy gold. It would be difficult, surely, to find a handsomer bird, but the Thrush, with his lovely speckled breast, is just as handsome. Then the Robin with *his* crimson breast, and his little round ball of a body—what bird could be prettier? Or the Chaffinch, or Greenfinch, or Linnet? Or the Bullfinch, surely *he* is handsomer than all of them (except the star-bird), with his beautiful mauve-peach-cherry-crimson breast, and his coal-black head and nice fat beak, and that pleasant, saucy look that he has. Yes, *he* is the handsomest, unless—oh, just fancy! we were actually leaving out the Goldfinch. *He* has crimson on each side of his face, and a black velvet cap on his head, whilst on both his wings he has feathers of a beautiful, bright, golden yellow. I think *he must* be the handsomest, unless it is the Brambling, who is dressed all in russet and gold. And then there is the Yellow-Wagtail! Could one think of a prettier little bird than he is—unless one tried a good deal? To be a wagtail at all is something, but to be not only a Wagtail but yellow all over as well, *that does* make a pretty little bird! And I daresay you have seen him running about on your lawn, too, at the same time as the thrush and the blackbird. And there is *another* bird, one that you do not see running or hopping over your lawn, but flying over it, sometimes far above it, when the sky is blue and the insects are high in the air, sometimes just skimming it when it is dull and cloudy and the insects are flying low. You know what bird it is I mean, now—the Swallow. I need not *say* how beautiful *he* is.

So, as you have seen all these pretty birds, and a good many others too—at least if you live in the country and not in London—perhaps you think that there cannot be many, or perhaps any, that are so *very* much prettier. Ah, but do not be too sure about that. You must never think that because something is very beautiful there can be nothing still more beautiful. *You* may not be able to imagine anything more beautiful, but that may be only because your imagination is not strong enough to do it. It may be a very good imagination in its way, better than mine perhaps, or a great many other people's, but still it is not good enough. In fact there is not one of us who has an imagination which *is* good enough to do things like that. *We* could never have imagined birds which are still more beautiful than those we have been talking about. Indeed we could never have imagined those that we *have* been talking about. Only Dame Nature has been able to imagine them both.

*She* can imagine anything, and the funny thing is that as she imagines it, there it is—just as if she had cut it out with a pair of scissors. Perhaps she does do that. She is a lady—*Dame* Nature, you know—so she would know how to use a pair of scissors. But what *her* scissors are like and how she uses them and what sort of stuff it is that she cuts things out of, those are things which nobody knows. Only, there are the birds, not only the beautiful ones that you have seen, but a very great many others which you have never seen, and which are so very much more beautiful than the ones you have, that if you were to see those beside them, they would look quite—well no, not ugly—thrushes and blackbirds and swallows and robin-redbreasts could not look *that*—but insignificant—in comparison.

Now it is about some of those birds—the very beautiful birds of all, the most beautiful ones in the whole world—that I am going to tell you; but all the while I am telling you, you must remember that they—these very beautiful birds—do not sing, whilst *our* birds—the insignificant-looking ones—do. So you must not think poorly of our birds because their colours are plain or even dingy—I mean in comparison with these other ones—for if they have not the great beauty of plumage, they have the great beauty of song. And perhaps you would not so very much mind growing up plain, like a lark or a nightingale (which would not be so very, very plain), if you could *sing* like a lark or a nightingale—as perhaps one day you will.

Indeed, I sometimes wish that those very beautiful birds were not quite so beautiful as they are. You will think that a funny wish to have, but there is a sensible reason for it, which I will explain to you. Perhaps if they were not quite so beautiful, not quite so many of them would be killed. For, strange as it may seem to you—and I know it *will* seem strange—it is just because the birds *are* beautiful that hundreds and hundreds, yes, and thousands and thousands, of them are being killed every day. Yes, it is quite true. I wish it were not, but I am sorry to say it is. People kill the birds *because* they are beautiful. But is not that cruel? Yes, indeed it is, very, very cruel. It is cruel for two reasons: first, because to kill them gives them pain; and secondly, because their life is so happy. Can anything be happier than the life of a bird? Surely not. Only to fly, just think how delightful that must be, and then to be always living in green, leafy palaces under the bright, warm sun and the blue sky. For I must tell you that these birds we are going to talk about live where the trees are always leafy, where the sun is always bright and the sky always blue. So they are always happy. Even if a bird *could* be unhappy in winter—which I am not at all sure about—there is no winter there. Now the happier any creature is the more cruel it is to kill it and take that happiness away from it. I am sure you will understand that. If you were carrying a very heavy weight, which tired you and made you stoop and gave you no pleasure at all, and some one were to come and take it away from you, you would not think that so very cruel. You would have nothing now, it is true, but then all you *had* had was that weight, which was so heavy and made you stoop. But, now, if you were carrying a beautiful bunch of flowers which smelt sweetly and weighed just nothing at all, and some one were to take *that* away, you would think *that* cruel, I am sure. A bird's life is like that bunch of flowers. How cruel, then, it must be to take it away from any bird. We should think it very wrong if some one were to kill *us*. Yet it is not *always* a bunch of flowers that *we* are carrying.

So, as it is cruel to kill the birds, and as they are not nearly so beautiful when they are dead as they are when they are alive, and as the world is full of tender-hearted women to love them and plead for them and to say, "Do not kill them," perhaps you will wonder why it is that they are killed. I will tell you how it has come about. When Dame Nature had imagined all her beautiful birds, and then cut them out of that wonderful stuff of hers—the stuff of life—with her marvellous pair of scissors, she said to her eldest daughter—whose name is Truth—"Now I will leave them and go away for a little, for there are other places where I must imagine things and cut them out with my scissors." Truth said, "Do not leave the birds, for there are men in the world with hard hearts and a film over their eyes. They will see the birds, but not their beauty, because of the film, and they will kill them because of their hearts, which are like marble or rock or stone." "They are, it is true," said Dame Nature, "and indeed it was of some such material that I cut them out. I had my reasons, but you would never understand them, so I shall not tell you what they were. But there are not only my men in the world; there are my women too. I cut *them* out of something very different. It was soft and yielding, and that part that went to make the heart was like water—like soft water. I made them, too, to have influence over the men, and I put no film over *their* eyes. *They* will see how beautiful my birds are, and they will know that they are more beautiful alive than dead. And because of this and their soft hearts they will not kill them, and to the men they will say, 'Do not kill them,' and my beautiful birds will live. Women will spare them because they have pity, and men because women ask them to. And to make it still more certain, see yonder on that hill sits the Goddess of Pity. She has come from heaven to help me, and has promised to stay till I return. It is from her that pity goes into all those hearts that have it, and because she is a goddess, she sends most of it into the hearts of women. Have no fear, then, for until the Goddess of Pity falls asleep my birds are safe." "But *may* she not fall asleep?" said Truth. But Dame Nature had hurried away with her scissors, and was out of hearing.

As soon as she was gone, there crept out of a dark cave, where he had been hiding, an ugly little mannikin, who hated Dame Nature and her daughter Truth, and did everything he could to spite them both. Their very names made him angry. He was a demon, really, and ugly, as I say. But he did not *look* ugly, because nobody saw him. All that people saw when they looked at him was a suit of clothes, and this suit of clothes was so well made and so fashionable, and fitted him so well, that they always thought the ugly demon inside it was just what he ought to be. So, of course, as every one had different ideas as to what he ought to be, he seemed different to different people. One person looked at the clothes, and thought him quite remarkable, another one looked at them and thought him ordinary and commonplace, and so on. Only every one was pleased, because, whatever else he seemed, he always seemed just what he ought to be. So, when two people both found that he was that, they each of them thought that he looked the same to the other. Of course the clothes were enchanted, really, only nobody knew it, and if any one had been told that it was the clothes and not the demon inside them they were looking at, he would not have believed it. It was only Dame Nature and her daughter Truth who could look at those clothes and see the little demon inside them, just as he really was. That was why he hated them, and never liked to hear their names.

This ugly little demon crept up to the Goddess of Pity, who looked at the clothes and was not even able to pity him; and, when he saw that he had her good opinion, he began to repeat a sort of charm to send her to sleep, for he knew that when once the Goddess of Pity was asleep he might do whatever he liked.

These were the words of the charm:—

> Fashion, fashion, fashion!
> Give a little sneer.
> Fashion, fashion, fashion!
> Science makes it clear.

Fashion, fashion, fashion!
A bird is not a bat.
Fashion, fashion, fashion!
Such a pretty hat!

Under the influence of this drowsy charm—which, of course, had no meaning in it whatever—the Goddess of Pity began to nod, and nodded and nodded till, on the last line, she went fast asleep, with a pleased smile on her face.

Then the wicked little demon took from one of the pockets in the suit of clothes that charmed everybody two little bottles that contained two different sorts of powders, one hot like pepper, and the other cold like ice, but both of them so fine that they were quite invisible. He took a pinch of the hot powder which was labelled "Vanity," and blew it upon the heads of all the women, and the instant it touched them they all looked pleased, and you could see that they were thinking only of how they looked, though they *talked* in a *very* different way. It was funny that they *all* looked pleased, because a great many—in fact, most of them—were plain, not pretty, and yet they looked pleased too, as well as the others. But, you see, it was all done by magic. Then from the other little bottle, which was labelled "Apathy," the demon took a pinch of the cold powder and blew it on the women's hearts, and as soon as it fell on them they became frozen, so that all the pity that had been in them before was frozen, too. Frozen pity, you know, is of no good whatever. You can no more be kind with it in that state than you can bathe in frozen water. So now there was nothing but vanity in the women's heads, and no pity in their hearts, and as the Goddess of Pity was fast asleep, it was not possible for any more to be put into them until she woke up. Nobody could tell when that would be. Gods and goddesses sometimes sleep for a long time, and very soundly. Besides, you know, this was a charmed sleep.

So, now, what happened after the wicked little demon had behaved in this wicked way? Why, the women whose hearts he had frozen began to kill the poor, beautiful birds, those birds that Dame Nature loved so, and had taken such pains to keep alive. I do not mean that they killed them themselves with their own hands. No, they did not do that, for they had not enough time to go to the countries where the beautiful birds lived, which were often a long way off as well as being very unhealthy. You see they were wanted at home, and so to have gone away from home into unhealthy countries to kill birds would have been *selfish,* and one should never be that. So instead of killing them themselves the women sent men to kill them for them, for *they* could be spared much better, and if they should not come back they would not be nearly so much missed. And the women said to the men, "Kill the birds and tear off their wings, their tails, their bright breasts and heads to sew into our hats or onto the sleeves and collars of our gowns and mantles. Kill them and bring them to us, that you may think us even more lovely than you have done before, when you compare our beauty with theirs and find that ours is the greater. Let us shine down the birds, for they are conceited and think themselves our rivals. Then kill them. Kill, kill, kill, kill, kill them." Then the men, whose hearts had always been hard, and over whose eyes there was a film, went forth into the world and began to kill the poor, beautiful birds wherever they could find them.

Everywhere the earth was stained with their blood, and the air thick with floating feathers that had been torn from their poor, wounded bodies. It was full, too, of their frightened cries, and of the wails of their starving young ones for the parents who were dead and could not feed them any more. For it is just at the time when the birds lay their eggs and rear their young ones that their plumage is most beautiful—most exquisitely beautiful—and it was just this most *exquisitely* beautiful plumage that the women, whose hearts the wicked little demon had frozen, wanted to put into their hats. They knew that to get it the young fledgling birds must starve in their nests. But they did not mind that now, their hearts were frozen and the Goddess of Pity was asleep.

So the birds were killed, and the lovely, painted feathers that had lighted up whole forests or made a country beautiful, were pressed close together into dark ugly boxes—or things like boxes—called "crates" (large it is true, but not *quite* so large as a forest or a country), and then brought over the seas in ships, to dark, ugly houses, where they were taken out and flung in a great heap on the floor. Soon they were sewn into hats which were set out in the windows of milliners' shops for the women with the frozen hearts to buy. You may see such hats now, any time you walk about the streets of London—or of Paris or Vienna, if you go there—for the Goddess of Pity is still sleeping, she has not woken up yet. There you will see them, and outside the window, looking at them—sometimes in a great crowd—you will see those poor women that the demon has treated so badly. There they stand, looking and looking, ravenous, hungry—you would almost say they were—longing to buy them, even though they have new ones of the same sort on their head. Ah, if they could see those birds as they looked when they were shot, before they were dressed and cleaned and made to look so smart and fashionable! If they could see them with the blood-stains upon them, the wet, warm drops running down over the bright breasts—perhaps onto the little ones underneath them—the poor, broken wings dragging over the ground and trying to rise into the air, through which they had once flown so easily, the flapping, the struggling! If they could see all this, and much more that had been done—that *had* to be done—before there was that nice, gay, elegant shop-window for them to look into, would it not be different then, would not the vain heads begin to think a little and the frozen hearts to melt? No, I do not think so, because of the ugly little demon in the correct suit of clothes. They would look in at the window and go in at the door still, and—shall I tell you something?—it would be the same, just the same, if all those bright feathers in every one of the hats had been stripped, not from the birds' but from the *angels'* wings. Those who could wear the one could wear the other, and if angels were to come down here I should not wonder if angel-hats were to get to be quite the fashion. Only first, of course, angels would *have* to come down here. I do not think they are so *very* likely to.

And the worst of it is that not only the *pretty* women wear the beautiful birds in their hats, but the plain ones do too, which makes so many more of them to be killed. If it was *only* the pretty women who wore them it would not be quite so bad, but the wicked little demon was much too clever to arrange it like that. He did not wish any of the birds to escape, and I cannot tell you how many *millions* of them *would* escape if only the pretty women were to wear their feathers.

But now, how are the birds to be saved—for *we* want them *all* to escape—and how are the women to be saved? That is another thing. You know it is not *their* fault. They were kind and pitiful till the wicked little demon blew his powder into their hearts. It is *his* fault. You may be angry with *him* as much as you like, but you must not think of being angry with the women. Indeed, you should be sorry for them, more even than for the birds, for it is much worse to be a woman with a frozen heart than to be a bird and be shot. Oh, poor, frozen-hearted women, who *would* be so kind and so pitiful if only they were allowed to be, if only the wicked little demon would go away, and the Goddess of Pity would wake up!

Then is there no way of saving them both, the poor birds and the poor women? Yes, there is a way, and it is you—the children—who are to find it out. Listen. It is so simple. All you have to do is to ask these women (these *poor* women) *not* to wear the hats that have feathers, that have birds' lives in them, and they will not do so any more. They will listen to you. There is nobody else they would listen to, but they will to you—the children. Perhaps you think that funny. Listen and I will explain it. When the wicked little demon blew his powder called "Apathy" into the hearts of the women, it froze them all up, as I have told you, but there was just one little spot in every one of their hearts that it was not able to freeze. That was the spot called Motherly Love, which every woman has in her heart, and which is the softest spot of all, if only a little child presses it—and especially if it is her own little child. So I want you—the little children who read this little book—to press that spot and to save the birds from being killed. Nobody can do it but you, nobody even can find that spot except you, but you will find it directly. And you are to press it in this way. Throw, each one of you, your arms round your mother's neck, kiss her and ask her not to kill the birds, not to wear the hats that make the birds be killed. And if you do that and really mean what you say, if you are really sorry for the birds and have real tears in your eyes (or at least in your hearts), then your mother will do as you have asked her, for you will have pressed that spot, that soft spot, that spot that even the wicked little demon, try as he might, could not freeze, could not make hard. And as you press it, the whole heart that has been frozen will become warm again, and the powder of the demon will go out of it, and the Goddess of Pity will wake up. You will do this, will you not? It is only asking, and what can be easier than to ask something of your mother? But you must make her promise. Never, never leave off asking her till you have got her to promise.

And if some of you have mothers who do not kill the birds, who do not wear the hats that have birds' lives sewn into them, well it will do them no harm to promise too. Then they never *will* wear them, and if they should never mean to wear them, they will be all the more ready to promise not to. Only in that case you might put your arms round the neck of some other woman that you have seen wearing those hats and kiss *her* and ask *her* to promise. And she will, you will have touched that spot because you are a little child, even though you are not her own little child. Perhaps you will remind her of a little child that was hers once.

Now I am going to tell you about some of the most beautiful birds that there are in the world, but you must remember that they are being killed so fast every day that, unless you get that promise from your mother very quickly, there will soon be no more of them left; as soon as she promises it will be all right, for of course it will not be only *your* mother who will have promised, but the mother of every other little girl all over the country, and as the birds were only being killed to put into their hats, they will be let alone now, for now no more hats like that will be wanted. No one will wear hats that have birds' lives sewn into them, any more.

So the beautiful birds will go on living and flying about in the world and making *it* beautiful, too. You will have saved them—*you* the children will have saved them—and no grown-up person will have done *anything* to be more proud about. I daresay a grown-up person *would* be more proud about what he had done, even if it was nothing very particular; but *that* is another matter.

Now we will begin, and as we come to one bird after another, you shall make your mother promise not to wear it in her hat.

# CHAPTER II

## BIRDS OF PARADISE

First I will tell you about the Birds of Paradise. You have heard of them perhaps, and how beautiful they are, but you may have thought that birds with a name like that did not live here at all. For the Emperor of China lives in China, and if the Emperor of China lives in China, the Birds of Paradise ought, one would think, to live in Paradise. But that is not the case—not now at any rate. They live a very long way off, it is true, right over at the other side of the world, but it is not quite so far off as Paradise is. No, it cannot be there that they live, because if you were to leave England in a ship and sail always in the right direction, you would come at last to the very place, instead of coming right round to England again, which is what you would do if you were to sail for Paradise—for you know, of course, that the earth is round. But why, then, are they called Birds of Paradise if they live here on the earth? Well, there are two ways of explaining it. I will tell you first one and then the other, and you can choose the way you like best. The first way is this.

A long time ago—but long after the little demon had crept out of his cave—the early Portuguese voyagers (whom your mother will tell you about), when they came to the Moluccas to get spices, were shown the dried skins of beautiful birds which were called by the natives "Manuk dewata," which means "God's birds." There were no wings or feet to the skins, and the natives told the Portuguese that these birds had never had any, but that they lived always in the air, never coming down to settle on the earth, and keeping themselves all the while turned towards the sun. One would have thought they must have wanted wings, at any rate, to be always in the air, but that is what the natives said. So the Portuguese, who did not quite know what to make of it, called them "Passaros de Sol," which means "Sun-birds" or "Birds-of-the-Sun," because of their always turning towards him. Some time after that, a learned Dutchman who wrote in Latin (just think!), called these birds "Aves Paradisei"—Paradise Birds or Birds of Paradise—and he told every one that they had never been seen alive by anybody, but only after they had fallen down dead out of the clouds, when they were picked up without wings or feet, and still lying with their heads towards the sun in the way they had fallen. So, after that these wonderful birds were always called "Birds of Paradise." That is one way of explaining how they got their names, but the other way, and perhaps you will think it a *little* more probable, is this.

Once the Birds of Paradise were really Birds of Paradise, for they lived there and were ever so much more beautiful than they are now, though perhaps, if you were to see them flying about in their native forests, you would hardly believe that possible. That is because you cannot imagine *how* beautiful *real* Birds of Paradise are, for these Birds of Paradise were not more beautiful than the other ones that lived there. All were as beautiful as each other though in different ways, and it was just that which made these Birds of Paradise discontented. "If we go down to earth," said they, "the birds of all the world will do homage to us on account of our superior beauty, for there will be none to equal us. So we shall reign over them and be their King. Here we are only like all the others. None of them fly to the tree on which we are sitting to do us homage." "Do not be foolish," said the tree (for in Paradise trees and all can speak). "The homage which you desire you would soon weary of, and the beauty which you enjoy here would, on earth, be only a pain to you, for it would remind you of the Paradise you had left but could never enter again. For those who once leave Paradise can never more return to it. Therefore be wise and stay, for if you go you will repent, but then it will be too late." And all the birds around said, "Stay," and then they raised their voices, which were lovelier than you can imagine, in a song of joy—of joy that they were in Paradise and not on earth. And the Birds of Paradise sang too, their voices were as sweet as any, but they had envy and discontent in their hearts. "Our singing cannot be surpassed, it is true," thought they, "but it is equalled by that of every other bird. We sing in a chorus merely. It would not be so on earth. We should be 'prima donnas' there." (Your mother will tell you what a prima donna is as well as what doing homage means.)

So, when the song was over, they flew to the Phenix, who was the most important and powerful bird of all the birds that were in Paradise. I have told you that all the birds there were equal, and so they were, only, you see, the Phenix was a little *more* equal than the others. One cannot be a Phenix for nothing. Now it was only the Phenix who could open the gate of Paradise, and let any bird in or out of it. He was not obliged to let them in, and there were very few birds (who were not there already) that he ever did let in. Many and many a bird fluttered and fluttered outside the door, that had to fly away again. But if a bird that was in Paradise wanted to go out of it, then the Phenix had to open the door and let it out, because if it had stayed it would have been discontented, and birds that are discontented cannot stay in Paradise. It would not be Paradise for long if they could. So when the Birds of Paradise said to the Phenix, "Let us out, for we are tired of being here, where all are equal, and wish to be kings and 'prima donnas' on earth," he had to do it, only he warned them as the tree had done, that if they once left Paradise they could never come back to it again. "The door of Paradise," said he, "may be passed through twice, but only entered once. When you pass through it the second time, it is to go out of it, and when you are once out of it, out of it you must remain. You can never come in again; you can only flutter at the gate."

"We shall never do that," said the proud Birds of Paradise. "We shall stay down on earth and be kings and 'prima donnas' amongst the other birds." So the Phenix let them out, and they flew down through the warm summer sky, looking like soft suns or trembling stars or colours out of the sunrise or sunset, they were so beautiful.

Then the birds of earth flew around them and did them homage, and, when they sang, the nightingale stood silent and hid her head for shame, and would never sing in the daytime any more, but only at night when the beautiful strangers were asleep. That is why the nightingale sings by night and not by day—only since the Birds of Paradise have lost their voice (which I am going to tell you about) she does sing in the daytime sometimes, just a little.

So the Birds of Paradise were kings and "prima donnas" amongst the birds of earth, and they were happy—for a time. They were not quite so happy after a little while, for they got tired of hearing the birds praise them, and, wherever they looked, they saw nothing to give them pleasure. The earth, indeed, was beautiful, but they remembered Paradise, and that made it seem ugly. There was nothing for them to see that was worth the seeing, or to hear that was worth the listening to, except their own beauty and their own song. But that reminded them of Paradise, and they could not bear to be reminded of it now that they had lost it for ever. In fact they were miserable, and it was not long before they were all fluttering outside the gates of Paradise, and begging the Phenix to let them in. But the Phenix said, "No, I cannot. I warned you that the gates of Paradise could only be passed twice, once in and once out, and then no more. I tried to keep you from going, but you chose to go, and now you must stay outside. You can never enter Paradise again." "If we cannot enter it," said the poor Birds of Paradise, "let us at least forget it. Take away our beautiful voices, so that, when we sing, we shall not think of all the joys we have lost. Let our song be no more than the lark's or the nightingale's, or make us only able to twitter, and not sing at all. Then we can listen to the lark and the nightingale, and perhaps, in time, we may grow to admire them. As it is, we must either sing or be silent. We do not like to sit silent, and when we sing we think only of Paradise." "Yes," said the Phenix, "I will take your voice, your beautiful voice of song." So he took it, and that is why the Birds of Paradise never sing at all now, not even as the lark and the nightingale sing.

After that they were happier, but still they had their great beauty, their glorious, glorious plumage, and when they looked at each other they felt sad and hung their heads, for still they thought of Paradise. "You have taken our song from us," they said (for they were soon there at the gate again), "but still our beauty remains. Take that also, that, when we look at each other, we may not think of the Paradise we have lost, and be wretched." "Fly back to earth," said the Phenix, "and when you are a little way off I will open the gates of Paradise wide, and the brightness that is in it will stream out and scorch your feathers, and you will be beautiful no more. Only you must fly fast, and you must not turn to look, for if you do, the brightness will blind you. You could bear it once when you lived in it and had known nothing else, but now that you have lived on earth you cannot. It would only blind you now." So the Birds of Paradise flew towards the earth, and, when they had got a little way, the Phenix opened the gates (he had only been speaking to them through the keyhole), and, as the splendour of Paradise streamed forth and fell upon them, their feathers were scorched in its excessive brightness, all except a few tufts and plumes which were not quite destroyed, because, you see, they were getting farther away every second. A little of their beauty was left, and that was enough to make them the most beautiful birds on earth (till we come to the Humming-birds), but they are very ugly compared to what they once were when they lived in Paradise. Think then, what the real Birds of Paradise must be like when those that have left it, and have had their plumage scorched and spoilt, are so very beautiful. That is the other way of explaining how there come to be Birds of Paradise living on the earth, and I think you will say that it is the more sensible way of the two. For as for people having ever believed that there were birds who had no feet or wings, and that lived always in the air with their heads turned towards the sun, why, *that* does not seem possible. Nobody could have believed in a thing like that, but *here* is a *natural* explanation.

But now you must not think that the Birds of Paradise which are in the world to-day, are the very same ones that used to live in Paradise, and that had their feathers scorched. Oh no, you must not think that. Those old Birds of Paradise died (for, of course, as soon as they came to earth they became mortal, they had been immortal before), but before they died they had laid a great many eggs, and reared a great many young ones, and these young ones, as soon as they were grown up, laid other eggs, and the birds that came out of those eggs laid others, and so it has been going on for hundreds of thousands of years, right up to now. And *now*, if you were to ask a Bird of Paradise where it was he used to live, and why he had lost his voice and got his feathers scorched, he would not know one bit what you were talking about. In hundreds of thousands of years a great many things are forgotten, and the Birds of Paradise of to-day are quite happy. The earth is quite good enough for them, and if they were not shot and put into hats for the women with the frozen hearts to wear, they would have nothing to complain of. They have something to complain of now, but you must remember your promise, and then, perhaps, they will not be shot any more.

Now, the Birds of Paradise that live on the earth to-day do not live all over it, as they used to do in those old days when they could hear the lark and the nightingale. It is only a very small part of the world that they live in now — small, I mean, compared to the rest of it — and there are no larks or nightingales there. I will tell you where it is. Far away over the deep sea, farther than Africa, farther than India, farther even than Burma or Siam, there are a number of great islands and small islands and middling-sized islands, which lie between Asia and Australia, and all of these together are called the Malay Archipelago. The largest of all these islands, and the one that is farthest away too, is called New Guinea, and it is a very large island indeed, the largest, in fact, in the world after Australia, which, as you know, is so large that we call it a continent. Round about this great island of New Guinea, and not very far from its shores, there are some other islands which are quite tiny in comparison, and it is here, just in this one great island and in these few small islands near it, that the Birds of Paradise live. They do not live in any of the other islands of the Malay Archipelago, but only just here in the ones that are farthest away of all.

It would take you weeks to go in a steamer to where the Birds of Paradise live, and if you were to go, not in a steamer but in a ship with sails, it would take you longer still. But when you got there you would not see the Birds of Paradise flying all about, as soon as you went ashore out of the ship or the steamer, as you would see sparrows here. Oh no, Birds of Paradise are not so common as that, even in their own country. They do not come into the towns, like sparrows, either, but live in the great forests where people do not often go, and even when one does go into them, it is difficult to see them amongst the great tall trees and the broad-fronded ferns and the long, hanging creepers that make a tangle from one tree to another.

Ah, those are wonderful forests, those forests far away over the seas! Some of the trees have trunks so thick that a dozen men—or perhaps twenty—would not be able to circle them round by joining their hands together, and so tall that when you looked up you would not be able to see their tops. They would go shooting up and up like the spires of great cathedrals, till at last they would be lost in a green sky, not the real sky, the blue one—that would be higher up still—but a green sky of leaves made by all the trees themselves, and in this sky of leaves there would be flower-stars almost as bright and as beautiful as the real stars of the real sky. Then there are other trees that have their roots growing right out of the ground, and going up more than a hundred feet high into the air. At the top of them is the tree itself, going up another hundred feet, or perhaps more, so that the real tree— the trunk at any rate—begins in the air, and before you could climb it, you would have to climb its roots, which *does* seem funny. And there are palm-trees with long, tall, slender trunks, smooth and shining, crowned with leaves that are like large green fans; and rattan-palms, which are quite different, for instead of being straight, their trunks twist round and round the trunks of other trees, going right up to their very tops, and raising their own most beautiful feathery ones above theirs. Sometimes they will climb first up one tree and then down it again, and up another, and then down that, till they have climbed up and down several trees, all of them very, very tall. How tall—or rather how *long*—*they* must be you may think. We say that a snake is so many feet long, not tall, and these rattan-palms are palm-creepers, great vegetable serpents, that twist and coil as they grow, and hug the forest in their great coils, which are larger and more powerful than those of any python or boa-constrictor. A python or a boa-constrictor could not kill a *very* large animal, but the great palm-snakes will crawl up the largest tree, and crush it and squeeze it till at last it dies and comes thundering down in the forest, and then they will crawl along the ground to another, and hug that to death, too. Then there are tree-ferns, which are ferns that have trunks like trees, which are sometimes thirty feet high, with fronds growing from their tops, so broad and tall that a number of people could sit underneath them in their cool, deep shade, as if they were a tent. And there are wonderful flowers in these forests, such as you only see here in botanical gardens or in the conservatories of rich people, orchids and pitcher-plants, and others with Latin names that one forgets. Some of them are flower-trees, or tree-flowers, as high as the trees are, and with hundreds of large, crimson blossoms glowing out like stars from their trunks. When you come upon them all at once in the gloom of the forest, it almost looks as if some of the trees were on fire.

Other flowers are golden like the sun and grow all together in clusters, whilst others, again, grow on the branches of trees and hang down from them by long stalks which are like threads, each thread-stalk strung with flowers, as a thread is strung with beads. Only these flower-beads are as large as sunflowers, with colours varying from orange to red, and with beautiful, deep, purple-red spots upon them.

But if you had wings like the Birds of Paradise, and could fly over the tops of the trees that make the forest, and look down into a leafy meadow instead of up into a leafy sky, then you would see the most gloriously beautiful flowers growing in that meadow, just as the daisies and buttercups grow in the meadows that you run over, here. For flowers love the light of the sun, and they struggle up into it through the leaves that keep it out. To them the leaves are not as the sky, but as the clouds that shut the sky out, and as they are clouds that will never roll away (even though they may fall sometimes in a rain of leaves), the only thing for them to do is to climb up to them and pierce them, and see the sky, with the sun shining in it, on the other side. So whilst a few flowers stay in the shade below, most of them grow and struggle up into the light and air above, and they are all in such a hurry to get there that every one tries to grow faster than all the others. Ah! what a race it is, a race to reach the sun. You have heard of all sorts of races, and some, per- haps, you have seen; running-races, races in sacks, boat-races, horse-races (though those, I hope, you never have and never will see), but you never either saw or heard of a fairer, lovelier, more delicate race than a race of flowers to reach the sun. Think of it, all over those great, wide, far-stretching forests, forests stretching away like the sea, and only bounded by the sea! Think of all the millions of flowers there must be in them, with all their delicate shapes, and rich, fragrant scents and glorious colours, and then think of them all growing up together, each trying to be the first to see the sun. So eager they all are, but so gentle. There is no pushing, nothing rude or rough. But as the leaves grow thinner, and the light shines more and more through them, they tremble and sigh with joy, and one says to another, "We are getting nearer—nearer. I can see him almost; we shall soon be bathed in his light." And so they all grow and grow till at last they gleam softly through the soft leaves, and see the beautiful deep blue sky and the glorious, golden sun. Yes, that is a lovely race indeed—as anything to do with flowers is lovely—and it is a race upwards, to the sky and to the sun. Not all races are of that kind.

It is in forests like those that the Birds of Paradise live; and now that we know something about where they live, we will find out something about them.

# CHAPTER III

## THE GREAT BIRD OF PARADISE

The Great Bird of Paradise lives in the middle of the great island called New Guinea, and all over some quite little islands close to it which are called the Aru Islands. He is the largest of the Birds of Paradise, and perhaps he is the most beautiful, but it is not so easy to be sure about *that*. However, we shall see what you think of him. His body and wings and tail are brown. "What, only brown?" you cry. "That is like a sparrow." Ah, but wait. It is not *quite* like a sparrow. It is a beautiful, rich, *coffee*-brown, and on the breast it deepens into a most lovely, dark, *purple-violet* brown. There! That is different to being just brown like a sparrow, is it not? Then the head and neck are yellow, not a common yellow, but a very pretty, light, delicate yellow, like straw. Sometimes ladies have hair of that colour, and when they have, then people look at them and say, "What beautiful hair!" which is just what they themselves say, sometimes, when they look in the glass. These feathers are very short and set closely together, which makes them look like plush or velvet, so you can think how handsome they must be. What would you think if you were to go out for a walk and see a bird flying about with a yellow plush or yellow velvet head? But the throat is handsomer still. *That* is a glorious, gleaming, metallic green. Some feathers are called "metallic," because when the light shines on them they flash it back again just as a bright piece of metal does; a helmet or a breastplate, for instance. You know how *they* flash and gleam in the sunshine when the Horse-Guards ride by. At least, if you have seen the Horse-Guards, you do, and if you have not, well, I daresay you have seen it in a dish-cover or a bright coal-scuttle. But fancy feathers as soft as velvet, gleaming as if they were polished metal, but gleaming all emerald green as if they were jewels—emeralds—too! Then on the forehead and the chin of this bird—by which I mean just under the beak—there are glossy velvety plumes of a deeper green colour. The other is emerald. These are like the deep, lovely greens that one sees sometimes in the fiery opal or the mother-of-pearl. What jewellery! and out of it all flash two other jewels—the bird's two eyes—which are of a beautiful bright yellow colour to match with the yellow plush of its head. Then this bird has a pale blue beak and pale pink legs, and I am sure if he thinks himself very handsome, you can *hardly* call him conceited. For he would be handsome only with this that I have told you about; that would be quite enough to make him a beautiful bird without anything else.

But *has* he anything else—any other kind of beauty *besides* what I have told you about? Listen. The emerald throat and the yellow velvet-plush head and the blue beak and the pink legs are as nothing, nothing whatever, compared to the glorious plumes which this Bird of Paradise has on each side of his body. Oh, you never saw such plumes, and you cannot think how lovely they are. There are two of them—one on each side—and each one is made up of a number of very long, soft, delicate silky feathers, which are of an orange-gold or golden-orange colour, and so bright and glossy that they shine in the sun like floss-silk. Just where they spring from the body each one of them has a stripe of deep crimson-red, and, to-wards the top, they soften into a pretty pale, mauvy brown. Even one feather like that on each side would be beautiful—or one all by itself in the middle—but fancy a *plume* of them on each side, a thick plume too, though each feather is so slender and delicate—there are so many of them. They look lovely enough when they stream out behind as the bird flies, for they are twice as long as its whole body, so, of course, the two plumes come together and make one lovely large one that lies as softly on the air as the feather of a swan does on the water. The body, then, is almost covered up in all these soft feathers, so that it is just like looking at a flying plume with wings and a head to it.

Yes, they look lovely enough then, these glorious plumes; but sometimes they look lovelier still, and that is when the Great Bird of Paradise raises them both up above its back so that they shoot into the air like two golden feather-fountains that mingle together and bend over and fall in spray all around, only it is a spray of feathers—not a real spray—and, instead of falling, they only wave and dance. Such a glorious, plumy cascade! The bird himself is almost hidden in his own shower-bath, but the emerald throat and the yellow-plush head look out of it and gleam like jewels as he peeps and peers about from side to side to see if any one is looking at him. For, of course, the Great Bird of Paradise does not make himself so *very* beautiful just for nothing. When he shoots up his feather-fountains and sits in a soft, silky shower-bath, he does it to be looked at, and the person he wants to look at him most is the hen Great Bird of Paradise, for—do you know and *can* you believe it?—the poor hen Great Bird of Paradise is *not* beautiful. She has no wonderful plumes—she has no plumes at all—and out of all those splendid co-lours I have told you about—orangy-gold and emerald green and all the rest of them—she has only one, which is the coffee-brown. Now, of course, a nice rich cof-fee-brown is a very good colour, but still, by itself it is not enough to make a bird one of the most beautiful birds in the world. So when a bird is *only* coffee-brown, then, compared to a bird who has all those other colours and the most wonderful plumes as well, it is quite a plain bird. So a poor hen Great Bird of Paradise is quite a plain bird compared to her handsome husband, with his emerald throat and yellow-plush head and his wonderful orangy-gold plumes.

But, then, if the poor hen bird has no glorious plumes of her own, she is al-ways looking at them, always having them spread out on purpose for her to look at, and that must be very pleasant indeed. When the male Great Birds of Paradise wish to show their poor plain hens how handsome they are—just to comfort them and make them not mind being plain themselves—they come to a particular kind of tree in the forest, a tree that has a great many wide-spreading branches at the top, with not so very many leaves upon them, so that it is easy for them to be seen by the hens, who are sitting in other trees near, all ready to watch them. Then they raise up their wings above their backs, stretch out their emerald necks, bow their yellow heads politely to each other, and shoot up their golden feather-fountains, making each of the long, plumy tufts tremble and vibrate and quiver, as they droop all over them and almost cover them up. The plumes begin from under the wings—that is why they lift their wings up first so that they can shoot straight up and so that the hen birds may see the little stripes of red, which I told you about, and which look like little crimson clouds floating in a little golden sunset. How beautiful they must look! Perhaps there may be a dozen Great Birds of Paradise, all bowing their heads and quivering their plumes, on a dozen branches of the tree, whilst a dozen more will be flying about from one branch to another, so that the tree and the air are full of beauty. The air never had anything to float upon her softer or lovelier than those golden floating plumes, and no tree ever bore blossoms *quite* so beautiful as those wonderful golden Paradise-flowers. And both the air and the trees are happy. Both of them whisper, "Oh thank you, thank you, Birds of Paradise." Of course the Birds of Paradise are happy too. They are happy to have such beauty and to be able to show it to the hens, who sit hidden in the trees and bushes around, and *they* perhaps—the hens for whom it is all done—are happiest of all. Then it is all happiness—and beauty. Beauty and happiness, those are the two things it is made up of.

There are not so many things that are made up of just those two. Try and think of some. A party, perhaps you may say (only it must be a juvenile one), or a pantomime. Well, of course, there is an *enormous* amount of beauty and happiness at things of that kind; but is it *all* beauty and happiness? Not *quite* all, I think. Still I am sure you would think it a very unkind thing if somebody were to break up a party before it were over, or to stop a pantomime before the last act had been performed. You would think that cruel, I am sure. And now if you were looking at those beautiful, happy Birds of Paradise at *their* party or pantomime (I *think* it is as pretty as a transformation scene), and all at once, when they were just in the middle of it, first one and then another of them were to fall down dead to the ground, till at last half of them lay there underneath the tree and the rest had flown away, would you not think *that* a most cruel and dreadful thing? Where would be the beauty and the happiness now? It would all be gone. Joy would have been changed into sorrow, and beauty *almost* into ugliness—for a dead bird is *almost* ugly compared to a beautiful, living one. And life would have been changed into death—yes, and *such* life, the life of happy, lovely birds, of Birds of Paradise. And I think that if you were there and saw that happen—saw those beautiful birds fall down dead—*murdered*—all of a sudden—you would be sorry and angry too, and you would say that only a demon could have done so wicked a thing.

You would be right if you were to say so. It *could* only be a demon—that same little demon that I told you about who sang a charm to send the Goddess of Pity to sleep and then froze the hearts of the women with his bad, wicked powder. That wretched little demon who wears the magic suit of clothes, which makes him seem all that he ought to be, is always killing the poor Birds of Paradise, just when they are feeling so happy and looking so beautiful. He does not do it himself (any more than the women), for, as he could not be in more than one place at a time, he would not be able to kill a sufficient number to satisfy him, and besides he has a great many other things of the same kind, but more important, to do. So he makes his servants do it. That has always been his plan. He has servants all over the world, and you must not think that they are as bad as himself, for that is not the case at all. They are not bad, but enchanted, so that they do all sorts of bad things without having any idea that they are bad. In fact they generally think that they are the finest things in the world. The demon has all sorts of little bottles with different kinds of powders in them, one for every kind of servant that he wants. In his little private workshop they all stand in rows upon a shelf and every one has a different label on it, so that he knows which to take up in a minute. One is labelled "Glory," and has a powder in it of all sorts of different colours, scarlet, blue, green, white, and a little of it dirty yellow. The man on whom a grain of this powder falls will always be wanting to kill people, and the more he kills the better man he will think himself, and so, too, will other people think him. You may imagine what a lot of work the demon can get out of a servant like that. Another one is labelled "Justice," and whoever the powder in that falls on will go through life always saying what he doesn't believe, and trying to make other people believe it. Others are labelled "Patriotism," "Duty," "Culture," "Refinement," "Taste," "Sensibility," and so on (all which words your mother will explain to you). The demon chooses them according to the kind of thing he wants done, and all on whom any of the powders inside the bottles fall become his servants in different ways—very grand ways, too, they are often thought—and go on serving him and thinking well of themselves, and being held always in great honour and respect, all their lives.

Now you must not, of course, think that these bottles *really* contain the things that are written on their labels. No, indeed, they are *false* labels, for, you see, *these* bottles stand in the window where people can see them, the demon does not keep them in his pocket like those other two I told you of. So when people see them they think that they have good powders instead of bad ones inside them, and when the stoppers are taken out the powders fly into their eyes, and they are blinded and never know the difference. Almost every one is blinded, for the demon just stands at the window of his workshop and blows his powders through the world. It is not necessary for him to walk up and down in it sprinkling them about. That would be a long, tedious way of doing things. He just blows them, and he need never be afraid of blowing too much away, for his bottles are magic bottles and always full. Outside his window there is always a great crowd looking at the bottles and admiring them, whilst the demon stands there in his magic suit of clothes, and seems to every one to be just what he ought to be.

They say that somewhere else in the world there is a very beautiful house with a radiant angel inside it, and that there, in vases of crystal and diamond—or something like crystal and diamond, but very much more beautiful—are the real things which the demon only pretends to have in his ugly little bottles. Any one has only to step in and ask for them, and the angel will open the vase and shed the essence that is inside it into his very heart. But—is it not funny?—hardly anybody ever goes into that house, and the few who do cannot persuade others to follow them. I will tell you why this is. The beautiful house does not *look* like a beautiful house at all to most people, and the angel of light who sits in the open doorway seems to them to be only a shabbily dressed, unfashionable sort of person. Nobody sees his wings, or, if they do, they think wings are vulgar and out of date. It is the demon who is to blame for this. He has had time to blow his magic powders all about the world, and they have blinded people's eyes and made what is really beautiful seem mean and ugly to them—for the demon's powders can blind the eyes as well as freeze the heart. But the little workshop of the demon, which is really as mean and wretched a place as you could find, *that* people think glorious and beautiful, and his ugly bottles are to them as vases of crystal and diamond. So they crowd about the demon's workshop, thinking it to be the angel's house, and into the angel's house they never go, for they think a demon—or at least an unfashionably dressed person with wings—which are out of date—lives there.

Now, it is one of those bottles with the false labels which the demon takes when he wants one of his servants in that part of the world to kill the Great Bird of Paradise; for I don't think the men in those countries would much mind what the women said to them. I cannot tell you which bottle it is, but it is none of those that I have told you about. The label upon it is not nearly such a grand one, and the powder is of a much coarser grain, for the man that the demon is going to blow it at is only a poor savage, who is black and nearly naked, and who is not able to serve him in such important ways as are people of a lighter colour and less scantily dressed. He is only fit to do little odd jobs now and again, and his wages are very low in consequence. Even what he gets he is often not allowed to keep, for the demon's upper servants take them away from him, and he is not strong enough to resist. One of his odd jobs is killing the poor Great Birds of Paradise, and now I will tell you how he does it. Only you must not be angry with him, or even with the other people whose servant he *thinks* he is, though they are all of them *really* the servants of one master, that wretched little demon in the magic suit of clothes, which makes him seem nice to everybody, although he is so nasty. It is *he* you must be angry with, for it is he who does all the mischief, in the way I have told you. He gets people into his power; but, if you do as I tell you, perhaps you will be able to save them from him, and to save the poor, beautiful Birds of Paradise, as well as other beautiful birds, from being killed and killed until they are all dead. Think what a lot of good you will have done, then, to have kept such beauty safe in the world, when it might have been lost out of it for ever. Yes, and you will have done more good than that even, for you will have helped to wake up the Goddess of Pity, and when once she is awake there will be so much for her to do—for, ah! she has been asleep so long.

But, now, listen. I have told you that the man who kills the Great Bird of Paradise is black and naked and a savage. But he is not a negro, although he is rather like one. His hair is something like a negro's hair, but there is much more of it. In fact it is quite a mop, and he is very proud of it. He is a Papuan, and the islands that he lives in are called the Papuan Islands, and are a very long way from Africa, which is where the negroes live. He is a tall, fine-looking man, with a beautiful figure, and he looks very much better naked than he would do if he were dressed. And when I said that he was black, this was not *quite* true, because he is really brown, but it is such a very dark brown that it looks black, and when a man is such a very dark brown that he looks black, then people *will* call him a black man, so that is what we will call this Papuan. Now, this black man is very quick and active—which is what most savages are—and he can climb trees almost as well as a monkey. When he finds one of those trees where the Great Birds of Paradise have their parties, their "Sacalelies" (that is what *he* calls them, it is a word that means a dancing-party), he climbs up into it early in the morning, before it is daylight, and waits for them to come. It does not matter how tall the tree is (and this kind of tree is very tall), or how dark it may be, this naked Papuan savage climbs up it quite easily and without slipping, just like a monkey. He takes up with him some leafy branches of another tree, and with these he makes a little screen to sit under, so that the Birds of Paradise shall not see him. Besides this, he takes his bow and arrows to shoot the poor birds with, for he does not use a gun, which would make too much noise, and, besides, the shot would hurt the beautiful plumage. The arrows do not hurt the plumage as the shot would, because at the end of each one there is a piece of wood, shaped something like an acorn, but as large as a teacup, and the large end of it makes what would be the point of an ordinary arrow. When the poor birds are hit with that great, smooth piece of wood they are killed, because it hits them so hard, but their plumage is not hurt at all, for nothing has gone into the skin, or torn the feathers.

So the naked black man waits behind his screen for the Great Birds of Paradise to come, and as soon as they come and begin to spread their plumes, he shoots first one and then another of them with his great wooden arrows, and they fall down dead underneath the tree. And, do you know, they are so occupied in showing off their beautiful plumes, and so happy and excited as they spread them out and look through them, or fly like little feathery cascades from branch to branch, that it is not till quite a number of them have been killed (for the black savage does not often miss his aim) that the others take fright and fly away. Then the black man climbs down from the tree and picks up the poor, beautiful, dead birds and takes them to another man who is yellow and not quite so naked as he is, who gives him something for them, but not so much as he ought to. The yellow man cheats the black man, and, when he has cheated him, he takes the skins to a white man, who is quite dressed and civilised, and sells them to him, and the white man cheats *him* a good deal more than *he* has cheated the black man—for, of course, the white man is the cleverest of the three. (You see there are yellow men in those countries—called Malays—as well as black men, and a good many white men go there as well.) Then the white man puts all the beautiful skins that he has bought from the yellow man, as well as a great many others which have been brought to him from all the country and from all the islands round about, into one of those large kinds of boxes called "crates," that I have told you about, and it is put on board a ship where there are a great many others of the same kind, all full of the skins and feathers of beautiful birds that have been killed. And the ship sails to England, and then up the Thames to London, where the crates are taken out and put into great vans and driven away to the great ugly warehouses to be unpacked and laid on the floor there in a heap, all as I have told you. You know what happens to them then.

**PAPUAN SHOOTING BIRDS OF PARADISE**

And now I will tell you something funny that I daresay you would never have thought of, but which is quite true all the same. That great heap of brightly coloured feathers lying on the floor, to make which hundreds of thousands of the most beautiful birds in the world have been killed, and hundreds of hundreds of thousands of their young ones that would have grown up beautiful, too, have been starved to death in the nest—that great big heap of the loveliest plumage is not so lovely, not nearly so beautiful as one living thrush or one living blackbird or one living swallow or one living robin-redbreast. That is the difference between life and death. A live Bird of Paradise is hundreds of times more beautiful than a live blackbird or thrush or swallow or robin-redbreast, but when it is dead it is not so beautiful as they are. Its feathers are more beautiful, still, of course, but where are the *waving* feathers, the *floating* plumes, the bright eyes, the quick, graceful movements, and the flight—the glorious flight—of a bird. They are gone, they are gone for ever, and, in their place, there is only stiffness and deadness and dustiness. Oh never, never wish to see a dead Bird of Paradise in a hat, when you can see a living thrush or blackbird on the lawn of your garden, or a living swallow flying over it. And even if you can never see a living Bird of Paradise—as I daresay you never will be able to—what then?—what then? You cannot see everything, but have you not got an imagination (your mother, who has got one, will tell you what it is), and is it not better to imagine a beautiful bird flying about in life and loveliness than to see it dead? And the people who have these hats with the Birds of Paradise, or with other beautiful birds, sewn into them, how much do you think they really care about them? Do they ever look at them after they have once bought them? Oh no, they never do. Sometimes they look in the glass with the hat on—yes—but then it is only to see themselves *in* the hat, not the hat.

So now you know what kind of birds the Birds of Paradise are, and how very beautiful they are, and you know how gloriously beautiful the Great Bird of Paradise is, and how it is killed and not allowed to live and be happy, just because it is so beautiful. But now these Great Birds of Paradise live only in some quite small islands and just in one part of one large one, and although there may be a good many of them where they do live, yet if they are always being killed in that way, very soon there will be no more of them left. Then there will be no more Great Birds of Paradise in the world—for they do not live outside those islands—and when they are once gone they can never, never come again.

But do you not think that it would be a dreadful thing if such a bird as this— this beautiful Great Bird of Paradise that I have told you about—were to be killed and killed until it was not in the world any more? Of course you think it would be a dreadful thing, and I am sure that you would prevent it if you could. And you *can* prevent it—*now*—yes, *now*—and in the easiest way possible. All you have to do—only you must do it directly—is to put your arms round your mother's neck and make her promise never, never to wear a hat with the feathers of a Great Bird of Paradise in it. Of course she will promise, if you ask her in that way, and keep on, and when she once has promised you must not let her forget it. You must remind her of it from time to time ("Remember, mother, you *promised*"), and, es- pecially, when you hear her talking about getting a new hat. And when you have made her promise about herself, then you must make her promise never to let *you* wear a hat of the sort (of course when you are grown-up and buy your own hats you never will), or your sisters either. And if you have a sister very much older than yourself who buys her own hats, then you can make *her* promise too. Perhaps *that* will be less easy, but she will do it in time if you tease her enough about it and want her to read the book. And then if you can get any other lady to promise, well, the more who do, the better chance there will be for the beautiful Great Bird of Paradise. Only you must make your mother promise first—that is the chief thing—and, to do it, you must tell her all about the wicked little demon, with his powders and his charm to send the Goddess of Pity to sleep. So now go to your mother, go at once, do not wait, or, if your mother is out anywhere, you must only wait till she comes home again.

# CHAPTER IV

## THE RED BIRD OF PARADISE

Then there is another very beautiful Bird of Paradise which is called the Red Bird of Paradise. It is no use trying to find out whether he or the one I have just been telling you about is the most beautiful, because if somebody were to think that one were, somebody else would be sure to have a different opinion. But now I will tell you what this Red Bird of Paradise is like, and then you will know how beautiful to think him. You know those lovely plumes that I told you about, that the Great Bird of Paradise has growing from both his sides, under the wings, and how he lifts up his wings and shoots them right up into the air, so that they fall all over him, like two most beautiful fountains that meet in the air and mingle their waters together. Now the Red Bird of Paradise has those plumes—those feather-fountains—too, and he can shoot them up into the air and let them fall all over him, and look out from amongst them as they bend and wave, and think "How lovely I am!" just the same as the Great Bird of Paradise can. They are not so long, it is true, but then they are very thick, and of a most glorious crimson colour—such a colour as you see, sometimes, in the western sky, when the sun is flushing it, just before he sinks down for the night. People talk about a sky like that and call it a glorious sunset when they see it in Switzerland. One can see it here, too, if one likes, but it is not usual to talk about it or even to look at it, unless one is in Switzerland (your mother will tell you the reason of this). Fancy a bird that looks out of a crimson sunset of feathers—crimson, but with beautiful white tips to them! Crimson and white, that is almost more splendid than orange-gold and mauvy-brown; unless you like orange-gold and mauvy-brown better—it is all a matter of taste.

But there is another thing that the Red Bird of Paradise has, which the Great Bird of Paradise has not got at all. He has two little crests of feathers—beautiful metallic green feathers—on his forehead. Just fancy! Not one crest, merely, but two. One talks about a feather in one's cap (which, of course, a *bird* may have without its being wrong); but what is a feather in one's cap compared to two crests of feathers on one's forehead? And such crests! And, besides his crimson sunset plumes with their white tips and the two little lovely green crests on his forehead, this bird has two wonderful feathers in his tail; they are not feathers at all, really, that is to say, the soft part of them on each side of the quill, which we call the web, is gone, and there is only the quill left, but it is such a funny sort of quill that you would never think it was one. It is flat and smooth and shiny, and quite a quarter of an inch wide. In fact it looks like a ribbon, a beautiful, black, glossy ribbon, twenty-two inches (which is almost two feet) long.

These two wonderful ribbons—I told you there were two—hang down in graceful curves as the bird sits on the branch of a tree, first a curve out and then in and then out again, just at the tips, so that the two together make quite a pretty figure. Of course, when there is any wind at all, they float gracefully about and look very pretty indeed, and when the Red Bird of Paradise flies, his two wonderful ribbons float in the air behind him, just as if he had been into a linen-draper's shop and bought something, and flown out again with it, in his tail. And yet, to make these two pretty ribbons—which are feathers, really, though they do not look like them—the soft part of the feather, which is usually the pretty part, has been taken away, and only the quill, which is usually almost ugly by comparison, has been left. And yet they are so handsome. That is because Dame Nature is such a wonderful workwoman. She can make almost anything she tries to, out of any kind of material.

Now, I must tell you that the Great Bird of Paradise has two funny feathers like this in *his* tail too—feathers, I mean, without webs to them—only his ones have just a little web at the beginning and, again, at the very tips; all the part in between has none at all. These funny feathers of the Great Bird of Paradise are even longer than those of the red one, for they are from twenty-four to thirty-four inches long, and thirty-four inches, you know, is almost three feet. But then they are thin, not broad like ribbons, and the plumes of the Great Bird of Paradise are so long that they are a good deal hidden by them, and, sometimes, hardly noticed amongst such a lot of finery. I think that must be why, when I was describing the Great Bird of Paradise to you, I forgot all about them, which, of course, I ought not to have done. But we all of us make mistakes sometimes, people who write books just as much as people who only read them, although, of course, people who *write* books *ought* to be more careful.

In fact, a great many of the Birds of Paradise have these funny feathers, and some of them have more than two. If you look for page 77 you will see a picture of the King Bird of Paradise, who has two beauties. He is not one of the birds that I talk about in this book—there was no room for him—but that does not matter. He sent me his picture, and it will show you what these "funny feathers" are like. There *is* a Bird of Paradise that has twelve of them, but now I must finish talking about the Red Bird of Paradise. I have told you about the glorious crimson plumes that he has on his sides, and the two funny feathers, like ribbons, in his tail, and the double crest of beautiful emerald-green feathers on his forehead, but, of course, there are other parts of him besides these, and I must tell you what they are like too. His head and his back and his shoulders are yellow, as they are in the Great Bird of Paradise, but it is a deeper and richer yellow, not the light, straw-coloured yellow which *he* has and which is very pretty too (I am sure we should never agree as to which is the prettier of these two birds). His throat, too, is of a deep metallic green colour—you know what metallic means now—but those lovely green feathers go farther up, in fact right over the front part of the head—which is his forehead—so as to make those two sweet little crests which he has, and which help to make him such a very handsome bird. The rest of his wings and body, and his tail, except the two ribbons in it, are brown—a nice, handsome, rich, coffee-brown—

his legs are blue, and his beak is a fine gamboge-yellow. Ah, *there* is a beautiful bird indeed! What would you say if you were to see a bird that was yellow and green with crimson-sunset plumes, and with two long glossy ribbons in his tail, and two beautiful crests on his forehead, with blue legs and a gamboge bill, flying from tree to tree in your garden?

Ah, yes, if you were to see him like that he would be more beautiful than any bird that has ever been in your garden or that has ever flown about in the woods or fields all over England—for he would be alive then—alive and happy. But if you were to see him dead he would not be so beautiful as any of the birds in your garden—no, not even as the sparrows (which is saying a good deal), for the beauty of life would be gone out of him, and that is the greatest beauty of all. And even if he were in a cage—unless it were a *very* large one with a great many trees in it—he would hardly look as beautiful as a lark does when he sails and sings in the sky.

So, however beautiful this bird is, you must only want to see him flying about in the forests or gardens of his native land, if ever you go there. If you do not go there, then you must not mind, but you must try to imagine him, which is almost as good as seeing him, if you do it properly. But you must never want to see him in a cage that is smaller than a large garden with trees in it, or dead in a glass case or a hat. It is better that beautiful birds should be alive and you not see them, than that they should be killed or made miserable for you to look at.

Now you may be sure that if the poor Great Bird of Paradise is killed because he is so beautiful, so is the poor Red Bird of Paradise because *he* is. It is dreadful to *be* sure of such a thing, and it is all because of the wicked little demon, and the Goddess of Pity being asleep. When the wicked little demon has been driven away, and the Goddess of Pity has been woken up—and it is you who are going to wake her—then you may be sure that no beautiful birds will be killed, and that the more beautiful they are the less people will ever think of killing them. But that time is not come yet. It will not come till you have read this book right through and finished it.

Now you remember that the Great Bird of Paradise is shot with arrows by a naked black man with frizzly hair like a mop—a man that we call a savage, though, really, he is not nearly so savage as some men who wear clothes all over them. You see, where he lives it is very warm, so that he does not want clothes, and he looks very much better without them, for his black, smooth skin is very handsome indeed, and so is his frizzly hair. If you saw him you would think him a very nice, amiable person, for he is always laughing and springing about, and his white teeth do flash so and his eyes beam, and he looks very pleasant indeed. I think you would quite like him, so you must not despise him because he is not civilised like us; never despise people because they have a different coloured skin to your own and wear no clothes and are called savages. Perhaps we may be better than people like that, but remember that the angels are much better compared to us, than we are, compared to such people. But do you think the angels *despise* us? Oh no, you *could* not think that, so *you* must not despise the savages. Never despise any one, that is the best thing. Instead of doing that, try to find out what is good about them—there is sure to be something, and, often, it is something which *they* have and *we* have not. *Never despise.*

Well, it is this same naked, frizzly-haired Papuan who kills the beautiful Red Bird of Paradise as well as the Great one, but he does not do it with bows and arrows, but in quite another way, which I will tell you about.

The Birds of Paradise are all fond of fruit; they like insects and things of that sort too, but fruit they are *very* fond of. They like a nice ripe fig, and there are so many fig-trees in that country, both growing wild and in the gardens too, that when the figs are ripe they do not trouble to finish one before they begin another, but fly about from tree to tree, making a bite here and another there, out of just the ripest and nicest. That is a nice, delicate way of eating figs, *I* think, just to take a little and leave the rest. We are so greedy that we always eat the whole fig, but then *we* are not Birds of Paradise.

But now there is one particular fruit which the Red Bird of Paradise likes better than any other, much better, even, than a ripe fig. It is a fruit which I do not know the name of, in fact I am not quite sure that it has a name, except in some language which we would neither of us understand. But you know what an arum lily is, and in those forests that I told you of there is a kind of arum lily which climbs up trees, for there are climbing lilies there as well as climbing palm-trees. This climbing arum lily has a red fruit, and it is this red fruit which the Red Bird of Paradise thinks so exceedingly nice. It will go anywhere to get that fruit, and the naked black man with frizzly hair knows that it will; so he makes a trap for it with the very fruit that it is so fond of.

But besides the fruit, two other things are necessary for making this trap; one of them is a forked stick like the handle of a catapult, and the other is some string. The Papuan soon cuts the stick, either with a knife that he has bought of a white man, or with a sharp piece of stone or flint, and the string he makes from some creeper, or by rolling the inner bark of a tree between his hands. When he has done this he takes the fruit and ties it to the forked stick, then he climbs up a tree that he knows the Red Birds of Paradise come to perch on, and ties the stick, with the fruit fastened to it, to one of the branches. To do this he takes a very long piece of string, one end of which hangs right down to the ground, and he ties it so cleverly that he has only to pull the string for the stick, with the fruit on it, to come away from the branch, just as a sash that is tied in a bow will come undone when you pull one of the ends. Then the black Papuan climbs down from the tree, again, and sits underneath it with the end of the long string in his hand, all ready to pull it when the right time comes.

Sometimes it will not be long before a Red Bird of Paradise comes to the tree, sometimes the Papuan will have to sit there the whole day or even for two or three days, for he is very patient and will not go away till he has done what he came to do. All savages are like that; they are ever so much more patient than civilised people who wear clothes. But whenever the poor Red Bird of Paradise does come, he is sure to see the fruit, and then he is sure to fly to it, to eat it, and *then* he is sure to get caught in the string. For the string has a noose in it which gets round his legs, and the frizzly-haired man underneath, who is watching the Bird of Paradise all the time, just pulls the cord, and down he comes as well as the stick. You see he cannot fly very well with the stick fastened to him, and, however much he tries to, it is no use, for the black man has only to keep pulling the string.

That is how the poor Red Bird of Paradise is caught, and as soon as he has caught him the black frizzly-haired man kills him and skins him—I need hardly tell you that he does that, for you know in whose service he is. Then the black man takes the skin to a yellow man, who buys it of him and cheats him a little, and the yellow man takes it to a white man who buys it of *him* and cheats *him* more, and it all happens just the same as it did with the Great Bird of Paradise, until the skin is lying on the floor of the warehouse, with all those other beautiful skins of poor beautiful birds—all killed to be put into the hats of women whose hearts the wicked little demon has frozen. Is it not shocking? But you know how to stop it. You have only to make your mother promise—yes, *promise*—*never* to wear a hat that has the skin or any of the feathers of a Red Bird of Paradise in it. Make her promise this before reading the next chapter.

# CHAPTER V

## THE LESSER, BLACK, BLUE, AND GOLDEN BIRDS OF PARADISE

Now I have told you about two very beautiful Birds of Paradise, and in this chapter I shall tell you about some others; at least I shall try to tell you what they are like, because not so very much is known about their habits, what they do, or how they live. That is because they live in such wild parts of the world, in such deep, dense forests, and on such high, steep hills. Not many travellers have been into these out-of-the-way places, and those that have gone there, instead of trying to watch them and find out all about them—which would have been so interesting—have shot at them with their guns whenever they have seen them, and have either killed them or driven them away. It is not by killing birds or by driving them away that you can find out much about their habits.

It would be much better if these travellers were to take a good pair of glasses and were to sit down in the forests or on the hills and watch the birds through the glasses whenever they saw them; for with a good pair of glasses one can watch birds even when they do not come very near to one. Then we should know something about them, and the more we know about a bird or any other living creature the more interesting it becomes for us. One cannot be *very* interested in something that one knows nothing about, but as one begins to know even a little about it, it begins to get interesting directly. But then, why is it that the travellers who go out to these countries take guns with them instead of glasses, and shoot the birds—as well as other animals—instead of watching them? That is a question which I cannot answer. All I can tell you is that it is as I say, and I am afraid the wicked little demon has something to do with it. But now we must get on, and first we come to the Lesser Bird of Paradise.

The Lesser Bird of Paradise is something like the Great Bird of Paradise, only it is not quite so handsome and not nearly so big—which, of course, is what you would expect from its name. Where the Great Bird of Paradise is brown the lesser one is brown too, but it is a lighter brown, not such a nice, rich, coffee-coloured one as the other, and, on the breast, this brown colour does not change into a blackish-violet or a browny-purple as you know it does in the Great Bird of Paradise—it is brown there just the same. On the back, though, the Lesser Bird of Paradise is all yellow, so that here, if you remember, it has the advantage; but then the long plumes on each side under the wings are not *so* long as in the Great Bird of Paradise, and they have only just a tinge of orange in them, instead of being of the beautiful golden-orange colour that *his* ones are. The tips of them, too, are white instead of mauvy-brown, and the two funny feathers in the tail are much shorter than the Great Bird of Paradise's funny feathers.

**THE LESSER BIRD OF PARADISE**

But although the Lesser Bird of Paradise is not such a beautiful bird as the Great Bird of Paradise is, still it is a very beautiful bird indeed—what Bird of Paradise is not?—and as it is commoner than the other Birds of Paradise and easier to get, it is the one that is most often killed and put into the hats that the women with the frozen hearts wear; which is why I want you to jump up and throw your arms round your mother's neck and make her promise never, never to wear a hat that has a Lesser Bird of Paradise in it.

And now, what would you say to a Black Bird of Paradise? For there is one— yes, and such a splendid bird. "Oh, but," you will say, "if he is black he cannot be so *very* beautiful, for he cannot be of all sorts of beautiful colours like the other ones." But have you not heard of a black diamond? That is black, but *in* its blackness all sorts of wonderful colours are lying asleep, and sometimes they wake up and flash out of it, as the sun's rays do out of a dark, stormy cloud, and then they go back into it again and are lost, as the sun's rays are lost when the sun goes in. Yes, they are asleep, those colours, and whilst they are asleep the diamond is really black, but when they wake up and begin to gleam and flash, and sparkle, and shoot about, then it is not a *black* diamond any more, although we may call it so.

And there may be a dark, deep cavern, so dark and so deep that you would be quite afraid to go into it, especially at night. But some gipsies, who were not afraid, have gone into it and have lighted a fire, and the flames leap up and glimmer through the smoke, and then sink for a moment and shoot up again, and fall on the sides and roof of the cavern, and make a deep glow in its mouth, and flicker on the leaves of the trees outside, and send out long tongues of flame that make a red light in the air and lick the darkness off everything that they touch. That cavern *was* dark and black before the fire was lighted in it, and when the fire goes out it will be dark and black again, but it is not dark and black just now, whilst the red fire is burning.

Or it may be a dark night, very dark and stormy, so dark that it is difficult for people who are out in it to find their way, whilst people who only look out of the window, say that it is a pitch-dark night. But now the rain is beginning to fall, and it comes down faster and faster, and there is a muttering in the dull sky, and, all at once, a flash of lightning leaps out of the darkness, cutting it as though with a red, jagged knife, and for an instant it is day, and you see the leaves on the trees, and the rain-drops falling through the air, and the fields with haystacks standing in them, or rivers winding through them, and the distant hills, and the line where the earth meets the heavens. Then, all in a moment—almost before you can say "Oh," and quite before the great clap of thunder that follows the lightning-flash—it is night—deep, dark, black night—again. The night in which there is a storm like that is a dark night, but it is not dark when the lightning is leaping and flashing.

It is the same with this Black Bird of Paradise. At first when you look at him, all his plumage is of a deep, dark, velvety black, a lovely black, a beautiful, smooth, glossy black, a black that seems almost to gleam and to sparkle as if it were jewellery—black velvet jewellery you may call it, very handsome, very beautiful indeed. Still it is black, but all at once all the colours that have lain asleep in it—blues and greens, and bluey-greens and greeny-blues, and purples and indigos, and wonderful bronzy reflections—wake up together, and flash out of it like the sparkles out of the diamond, like the tongues of fire out of the black cavern, like the lightning out of the dark night. There they all are, flashing and leaping about, meeting and mingling, then shooting apart, playing little games with each other, till all at once they fall asleep again, and there is only the smooth, glossy black, the deep, jetty black, the shining, gleaming, satiny-velvety black, the black velvet, black satin jewellery. That is what a Black Bird of Paradise is like, like a black diamond, like a cavern with a fire lighted in it, like a dark night with flashes of lightning.

But now I will tell you a little more about his appearance, for this that I have told you is only just to give you an idea of how that wonderful material, from which Dame Nature with her scissors cuts out all her children (for all things that are alive are the children of Dame Nature), can be black, and yet have all sorts of colours in it at the same time.

First, you must know—so as not to make any mistake—that this "Black Bird of Paradise" has another name—indeed he has two other names, but one of them is in Latin, so we won't bother about that. There are some birds that have no English names, and when we come to them we will have to call them by their Latin ones—but as long as a bird has an English name we will never trouble our heads about what its Latin name may be, not we, any more than the bird itself does, and no bird that has an English name ever thinks about what its name is in Latin—in fact I really do not believe that it knows. An English name is enough for *any* bird, if only it is so *fortunate* as to have one. Now this bird is so fortunate as to have two English names—the Black Bird of Paradise, that you know about—which is what the English people who live in its own country call it—and the Superb Bird of Paradise, which is what naturalists at home in England call it. The *Superb* Bird of Paradise! Just fancy having a name like that! Supposing a gentleman—some friend of your father and mother, who calls sometimes at the house—were to be called the superb Mr. Jones or the superb Mr. Robinson! Only he would have to be very much more handsome than he is at all likely to be, before he would deserve a name like *that*.

Well, the two most wonderful things about the Superb or Black Bird of Paradise—after his marvellous black plumage, that has all sorts of colours lying asleep in it—are two wonderful ornaments that he has, one on his head and one on his breast. The one on his head is the most wonderful. It is a sort of crest—at least I think that is the best name for it. Some people, I know, call it a shield, but then that is what they call the other wonderful thing on the breast too; so, if they call that a shield, I think they should call this a helmet, for it is a helmet, and not a shield, that soldiers wear on the head. *I* shall call it a crest, but it is one of the most extraordinary crests that any bird ever had. It is like a pair of black velvet lappets, so long that they go all down the back and reach half-an-inch beyond the tips of the wings. But at the back of the head, where this crest begins, the two lappets meet, and they are joined together for a little way before they begin to go apart. I tell you what will give you an idea of the shape of this crest. Have you ever seen a pair of trousers that have been washed, and are hanging out on a clothes-line to dry, with the legs very wide apart, so wide they look as if they had been stretched?—I don't know if they really have. Of course you have seen such a thing. Well, that will give you an idea—mind, that is *all* I can say—of what this wonderful crest that is worn by the Black Bird of Paradise is like. The legs of the trousers are the two lappets, from where they are divided from each other, and, farther up, they join and become all one, just as the legs of a pair of trousers *do*. Only, of course, I need hardly tell you that a crest of beautiful, black, velvety feathers, glossed with bronze and purple, has a far more *elegant* appearance than a pair of trousers hanging out to dry, though it may have just a *little* the same shape.

Now I think you will agree with me that this crest is a wonderful thing, even when it is only lying down along the neck and body of the bird. But what would you say when you saw the Black Bird of Paradise lift it right up above its head?— which is what he does, you may be sure, when he wants to show off before the hen bird, who has no crest on *her* head nor shield on her breast, and whose black feathers, I am afraid, are not nearly so glossy and velvety, and have no colours lying asleep in them and ready to wake up all of a sudden. Ah, you would think the Black Bird of Paradise a wonderful, wonderful bird if you were to see him bowing politely to his hen and lifting up his wonderful, wonderful crest to her.

**KING BIRD OF PARADISE**

But I told you this bird had a shield too, and when he lifts up his crest over his head, he shoots out his shield in front of his breast, at the same time, and this shield is something of the same shape as the crest or helmet, only smaller, and always of a lovely bluey-green colour, with a glossy sheen upon it that is just like that upon satin. Yes, *always*, for the colours that go to sleep in the other parts of the Black Bird of Paradise's plumage, keep wide awake in the shield on its breast, or, if you ever do catch them napping, it is only just for a single instant, and then out they flash again, wider awake than ever. So now, if you were to say—as I am sure you would say—that the Black Bird of Paradise was a wonderful, wonderful bird, even if you were to see him with only his crest lifted up, what, ah, *what* would you say if you were to see him with his crest lifted up and his shield shot out at the same time? Why, I think that then you could not say less than that he was a wonderful, wonderful, *wonderful* bird—three wonderfuls instead of only two. And indeed you would be right.

Yes, he is a wonder, is the Black Bird of Paradise, though I must tell you that he has not any of those long, silky feathers that hang down like cascades and shoot up like fountains, from the sides of those other Birds of Paradise I have been telling you about. And he has no long "funny feathers" in his tail either. You see he cannot have everything, and his crest and shield are instead of those. They are not quite so beautiful, perhaps, but I think they are still more wonderful. Even when his crest—his helmet—is laid down and his shield is not stuck out, the Black Bird of Paradise is a wonder, but when he raises the one up and shoots the other out, both at the same time, and says to the hen, "Look at me!" and all the colours that have been asleep in the helmet, or awake in the shield, gleam and flash and sparkle together, ah, *then* he is a wonder of wonders.

Then, do you think he is a bird that ought to be killed and killed and killed, only to have those beautiful, bronzy-black crests, and satiny-green, gleaming shields of his set in hats where they soon get dull and dusty, and where he can never raise them up or shoot them out or pay proper attention to them—because he is dead, dead, dead? Is he to be killed and killed till he is gone for ever, and there is not one more beautiful Black Bird of Paradise in the whole world? Oh no, no, no; it ought not to be so—it must not, it *shall* not—because you will prevent it—yes, you. You will turn to your mother now, this minute, if she is there, if she is reading this to you, or, if not, you will run to her—oh, so quickly, so quickly—and ask her, beg her—keep on asking and asking, begging and begging her to promise—till she *has* promised—never, *never* to buy a hat that has a beautiful Black Bird of Paradise in it.

Now, as I have said that the Black Bird of Paradise is such a very wonderful bird—as I have even called him a "wonder of wonders"—perhaps you will think that there is no other Bird of Paradise quite so wonderful as he is. Well, I do not wonder at your thinking so; and, do you know, whilst I was describing him to you and telling you how wonderful he was, I thought so too. But I had forgotten the Blue Bird of Paradise.

The Blue Bird of Paradise is quite as wonderful as the Black one. Perhaps—but mind I only say perhaps—he is even a little more wonderful. To begin with, blue is a very uncommon colour for a Bird of Paradise to be of. None of the Birds of Paradise that I have told you about have feathers that are really blue. There are blue lights, I know, in some of their feathers, especially on the head, but still they are not quite blue. You could hardly call them blue feathers, for there is a green light or a purple light as well as a blue light in them, which makes them bluey-green or greeny purple, or, at any rate, green or purple *and* blue, not just blue by itself. And then, as you know, sometimes all those lights go to sleep and then the feathers are black. I do not think there is any Bird of Paradise except the Blue Bird of Paradise whose feathers are really and truly blue, and I am quite sure that there is no other one—at least that we know of—which has so much blue about it, that you would think of it as a blue bird, or that has blue feather-fountains—those wonderful long silky plumes that grow out of each side under the wings.

That is what is most wonderful in the Blue Bird of Paradise. There is no other Bird of Paradise that can sit under a blue fountain or look out of a blue sunset. But the plumes of the Blue Bird of Paradise are not so long as those of the Great or the Lesser Bird of Paradise, and when he spreads them out they go more on each side of him than up over his head, and, for this reason, I think, he looks more as if he was looking out of a sunset than sitting under a fountain. You have seen a beautiful sunset often; there will be blue in it somewhere, cool, lovely lakes or bays, or long, stretching inlets, of the loveliest, purest, most delicate blue. But the clouds that float in those bays and lakes like islands, or that shut them in and make their shores, like great burning continents, are not blue, but rosy red or fiery crimson or molten gold or golden-crimson flame. That, at least, is what the brightest ones are like, those that are gathered nearest round the sun. Now, if they could keep all their brightness and glowingness and be blue instead of rose or crimson or gold, then it would be a blue sunset; and that is what the sunset is like that the Blue Bird of Paradise looks out of, when he spreads out his plumes, just as the sunset that the Red Bird of Paradise looks out of, when *he* spreads out *his* plumes, is like a red sunset—only of feathers, of course. One is a blue feather-sunset, and the other a red feather-sunset.

And how soft those feathers are, those wonderful, blue sunset-feathers of the wonderful Blue Bird of Paradise. Oh, I cannot tell you how softly they droop down over his breast, or how softly—how *very* softly—each feather touches the other one, upon it. How softly, I wonder—for I know you will want me to say. As softly as a snowflake falls upon snow? Oh, more softly than that. As softly as two gossamers are blown together in the air? Still more softly, even. As softly, then, as your mother kisses you when you are asleep, and she does not wish to wake you? Yes, I think it is as softly, or almost as softly, as that. Those are two of the very softest kisses—when your mother kisses you when you are asleep, so as not to wake you, and when the soft blue feathers of the plumes on each side of a Blue Bird of Paradise, meet and kiss each other on its breast.

Now that is all I am going to tell you about the front part of the Blue Bird of Paradise—for those wonderful blue feathers that grow on each side become the front part of him when he spreads them out. You see, they open out like two fans, with the handles turned towards each other, and meet together on the breast and above the head, so as to make one large fan or screen. Of course there is something behind this screen, and through it peeps the head of the bird, which is very pretty too. But you don't look at his head, you don't seem to see it. All you see or look at are those beautiful, beautiful plumes, that lovely screen, that wonderful soft blue feather-sunset.

As for the back part of this wonderful Blue Bird of Paradise, well, that is blue too, most of it—a handsome blue, a lovely blue, a gleaming, shining, glossy, satiny blue that looks darker when you see it from one side, and lighter when you see it from another, and which gleams and glints and is very resplendent (which is a word your mother will explain to you) however you look at it. Oh, a glorious blue, a magnificent blue, but not *such* a blue as the blue of those soft lovely feathers that spread out on each side and curl over and meet and kiss each other so softly, on the breast. And the head and neck of the Blue Bird of Paradise (for sometimes he puts them behind the screen, and then they are the back part of him) are of a soft velvet brown that, as you look at it, becomes a soft velvet-claret-magenta colour (which your mother knows all about and will explain to you), and in his tail there are two long "funny feathers" that hang down from the bough he is sitting on, and—and *now* you must try to imagine him. *When* you have imagined him—or before you have, if you are not able to—you must make your mother promise—now what? You know, of course. You must make her promise *never* to wear a hat with a Blue Bird of Paradise's feathers in it.

Now we come to the Golden or Six-shafted Bird of Paradise, who lives just in one part of New Guinea—that long part at the north that goes out into the sea, and which we call a peninsula; you have only to look at the map and you will see it. Now I think of it, the Superb or Black Bird of Paradise—or shall we say the Superb Black Bird of Paradise?—lives there too, so I daresay they sometimes see each other. Perhaps they call on each other, for, you see, they are both of them distinguished. One is superb and the other golden, and when two people are like that they do not mind calling upon one another. You see, neither of them can be hurt by it then. A *superb* person may call upon even a *golden* person, and yet feel quite well after it, and it will not do a *golden* person any harm at all to call upon a *superb* person. So, if birds are like people, I feel sure that sometimes the Golden and the Superb Bird of Paradise call upon each other.

Now you will want to know why this Bird of Paradise is called both the Golden and the Six-shafted Bird of Paradise. Well, he is called the Golden Bird of Paradise because he has lovely golden feathers on his throat and breast, and he is called the Six-shafted Bird of Paradise because six little arrows—for that is what they look like—seem to have been shot into his head, three on each side—arrows, you know, are sometimes called shafts. These little shafts or arrows are six inches long—almost as long as the bird itself—and bend right back over his body, as far as to the tail. Of course each of them is really a feather—an arrow that is all feather—but it is a "funny feather" with only the quill, which is very thin and slender, till quite the end, where there is just a little oval piece of the soft web—the part that looks really like a feather—left upon it. That is what makes them look like arrows. But is it not curious that the "funny feathers" of *this* Bird of Paradise are in his head instead of in his tail? I think it must be because Dame Nature wanted to make him a little different.

Of course you will see at once that six feathers like that—to say nothing of his wonderful golden breast—make the Six-shafted (or Golden) Bird of Paradise quite as remarkable as the Black or the Blue, or any of the other, Birds of Paradise. Whether it makes him *more* remarkable, that I really can't say. *You* must make up your mind about that. The fact is, *all* the Birds of Paradise are remarkable. I am sure if they were all together in one place, and you were to say out loud that any one of them was the *most* remarkable, all the other ones would be very much offended.

But now, besides his six little shafts or arrows and the beautiful golden feathers on his throat and breast—they are very large, I must tell you, those feathers, and sometimes they look green and blue as well as golden—this Bird of Paradise has two immense tufts of beautiful, soft, silky feathers on each side of the breast. So large each tuft is, that when he lifts them both up—as of course he can do—they almost hide him altogether. Then on the back of his head he has a band of feathers, so wonderfully bright that they do not seem to be feathers at all. They look more like jewels—yes, jewels. It is as if some magician had taken the sheen and shining light out of the emerald and topaz, and put them on that bird's head, and told them to stay there. Then on his forehead, just above the beak—as if all this were not enough—there is a patch, quite a large patch, of pure white feathers that shine like satin. Really I think you might almost say that this Bird of Paradise was *the* most wonderful of all the Birds of Paradise. But take care, do not say it out loud or you will offend *all* the others. Only I forgot, they are not here. Well, then, you *may* say it out loud, if you really think so. I do wish I could have got this bird's picture, but as he would not give it me, you must look at the picture of the Golden-winged Bird of Paradise instead. *He* is a very handsome bird, too—very much brighter than he looks.

Well, this makes the sixth Bird of Paradise which I have been able to tell you something about—I mean about their appearance, for very little else is known about them. But, do you know, there are some forty or fifty different kinds, and, of course, if I were to describe them all, or anything like all (which, however, I should not be able to do), this little book would become quite a big book, and there would be no room in it for any other kinds of beautiful birds. So I won't describe any more Birds of Paradise, but I will just say something, before getting on to the other beautiful birds, about Birds of Paradise and beautiful birds in general. That means about most Birds of Paradise and most other beautiful birds. When we talk about things in general, or people in general, we mean most things or most people. But that must be in another chapter, for this one has been quite long enough, and so we must end it. Oh, but wait a minute. Really, I was quite forgetting. First you must get your mother to promise never to buy a hat in which there are any feathers belonging to the Golden or Six-shafted Bird of Paradise. Yes, and never to wear it either, even if she did not buy it, but had it given to her. Of course your father might give your mother a hat, but if he were to give her one of that sort, he would have to take it back to the shop and change it for another.

GOLDEN-WINGED BIRD OF PARADISE

# CHAPTER VI

## ABOUT ALL BIRDS OF PARADISE, AND SOME EX-PLANATIONS

As I have told you, there are some forty or fifty different kinds of Birds of Paradise, and they are all of them as beautiful, or nearly as beautiful, as those that I have described, each one in its own special way. Of course you must know yourself, or your mother will tell you, that all this wonderful beauty has not been given to these birds for nothing, and I have told you that the male Birds of Paradise, who alone have it, show it off to the poor hen birds, whose plumage is quite sober in comparison—though you must not think that *they* are not pretty birds too—because they are pretty, though in a quieter style. So they are not *really* "poor" hen birds, that is only just a way of speaking. They are happy enough, you may be sure, for they have their husbands' fine clothes to look at. But what is so interesting, is that each of these different kinds of Birds of Paradise has some different way of arranging and showing off his fine clothes—for, of course, a bird's feathers are his clothes just as much as our coats and dresses are ours. And, besides that, each one of them puts himself into some peculiar attitude, which he thinks is the best one to let his plumage be seen as he would like it to be. We may be quite sure of this, because it is what all birds do that have beautiful plumage; and many of them have regular places that they come to, to run or jump about in, just as soldiers come into a park or common to march about in it, and show off their nice pretty uniforms. There will always be a great many hen birds round these places, to look at the beautiful males, and there are always a great many ladies round the park or common, to look at the beautiful soldiers.

Now, would it not be interesting if we knew what all these different Birds of Paradise did, and how they arranged their plumage, and what attitudes they went into, and whether they ran or jumped or flew or did all three, and all the rest of it? If only there was somebody who knew all that, I think he could write a very interesting book, and if only some one would go out into those countries, with a pair of glasses (or even a pair of eyes) instead of with a gun, and whenever he saw a Bird of Paradise would just look at it through the glasses (or with his own eyes, if it was near enough) instead of shooting it, I think *he* might write an interesting book. I am sure *I* should find it interesting, and I *think* you would too. Depend upon it, if any one could tell people what a Bird of Paradise did, he would interest them very much more than by telling them how he shot it. That is not at all interesting, how he shot it. Do you think it would be so *very* interesting for people to know how you broke a very handsome ornament in your mother's drawing-room? Why, I don't think it would interest even your mother—much; but she would be very sorry you broke it. And that is just how *I* feel (and I think some other people do too) when a person tells me how he shot a Bird of Paradise. Things of that kind interest the little demon. If they interest any one else, I am afraid it is only *because* of that little demon, because of his wicked powders and his having sent the Goddess of Pity to sleep.

But I am sorry to say that there is hardly anybody who knows anything about all these Birds of Paradise, anything about their habits and how they live and how they dance and the way they arrange their wonderful plumage, so as to make it look as beautiful as possible. Perhaps there are a few people who know just a little—a *very* little—about some of the more common kinds, but as for all the rest, if any one knows anything about them, it must be those black or yellow people that we call savages, who live in the same countries that they live in. That is because, when a traveller from Europe goes out to those countries he always takes a gun— not glasses (or if he does take a pair of glasses he does not use them, or his eyes either, in the right way), and when he sees one of these rare Birds of Paradise, he shoots it, or else frightens it away, as I told you. Then, when he comes back, he writes his book and tells you how he shot it, or tried to shoot it, and then he says: "Unfortunately, nothing whatever is known of the habits of this species." It is not very wonderful that *he* knows nothing of them, is it? And yet this traveller, with his gun, almost always calls himself a *naturalist*. Now a *real* naturalist is a person who loves nature. But is not that a funny way to love her—to shoot her children? Depend upon it, that one of those little bottles that the demon keeps his powders in, is labelled "Natural History" or "Love of Nature." You know that *his* bottles have generally a false label on them.

So, I am afraid I cannot tell you much about what the Birds of Paradise do, or how they show off their beautiful feathers. Indeed, it is very much the same with most other beautiful birds, and for the very same reason that I have been telling you, because people *will* shoot, instead of looking and watching. Just the little that we know about the Great Bird of Paradise, how he has a special tree that he comes to, to have those dances that the natives call "Sácalelis," and how he flies about with his plumes waving, or sits underneath them as if he were in the spray of a falling fountain, that I have told you; but, besides this, I can only tell you just a very little about a Bird of Paradise that I have not said anything about, because, you know, there are so many of them. The little I can tell you is this. Two gentlemen—one of them a Mr. Chalmers and the other a Mr. Wyatt—were once travelling in the part of New Guinea where this Bird of Paradise lives, and one morning, when they were up early, they saw four of the cock birds and two of the hens, in a tree close by them. This is what one of these gentlemen says about them (if there is any word too long for you, or that you don't understand, you must ask your mother to explain it):—

"The two hens were sitting quietly on a branch, and the four cocks, dressed in their very best, their ruffs of green and yellow standing out, giving them a handsome appearance about the head and neck" (yes, I feel sure of that), "their long flowing plumes so arranged that every feather seemed combed out, and the long wires" (he means the "funny feathers") "stretched well out behind, were dancing in a circle round them." (Just fancy!) "It was an interesting sight." (I should *think* so!) "First one and then another would advance a little nearer to a hen, and she, coquette-like" (you will have to ask your mother what *that* means), "would retire a little, pretending not to care for any advances. A shot was fired, contrary to our expressed wish, there was a strange commotion, and two of the cocks flew away" (you see what shooting does), "but the others and the hens remained. Soon the two returned, and again the dance began, and continued long. As we had strictly forbidden any more shooting, all fear was gone; and so, after a rest, the males came a little nearer to the dark brown hens. Quarrelling ensued, and in the end all six birds flew away."

Fancy seeing all that! I think it is wonderful that any of the birds stayed after the shot had been fired, and if another one had been, no doubt they would all have gone. Those travellers, you see, were a little better than most travellers are. They did not kill the birds (perhaps *they* were *not* naturalists), and the consequence is they have had something interesting to tell us about them. Still, I think if I had been there I should have had a *little* more to say, and instead of just saying that the cock birds were dancing, I should have described *how* they were dancing, and what sort of attitudes they put themselves into. And I think I would have waited at that place, and gone to those trees again very early next morning, all by myself, to see if those birds came back to dance there. Still, what these travellers do tell us is very interesting, very much more interesting than if they had only written, "Here we shot," or "Here we obtained another specimen of Paradisea Something-elsea"—which, of course, would be the Latin name. Naturalists like to tell us the Latin name of the animals they shoot. If they only had an English name I don't think they would care nearly so much to shoot them. How sorry we ought to be that animals have Latin names!

But, now, how is it that it is only the cock bird—the male—of all these Birds of Paradise who is so beautiful, whilst the poor hen—the female bird—is quite plain, in comparison? Well, I must tell you, first, that this is not only the case with Birds of Paradise, but that it is just the same with other birds as well. In most, if not all, of the beautiful birds I am going to tell you about, it is the male bird that is so *very* beautiful, so that perhaps you will begin to think that this is the case with *all* beautiful birds, and that there is no hen bird that has *very* splendid or brilliant plumage. But this is not so at all. You would make a great mistake if you were to think that. In most of the parrots—those brightly-coloured birds that you know so well—the male and female are alike, and if you were to see a kingfisher—the star-bird that I told you about in the first chapter—gleaming and glancing up a river, you would not know whether it was the one or the other. The feathers of the female scarlet flamingo are almost—if not quite—as scarlet as those of the male; the cock robin's breast is not more red than the breast of the hen robin, at least you would find it difficult to tell the difference; male and female pigeons—and some of them are very splendid—are as bright as each other, and so it is with a very great number of other birds.

Now does not this seem funny, that some male birds should be so much handsomer than their wives, whilst some *hen* birds should be just as handsome as their husbands? Is there any way of explaining this, or, rather, do we know how to explain it? for there *is* a way of explaining everything—a right way, I mean, of course. The difficult thing is to find it out. Well, there are some clever people who have been thinking about this funny thing, and they try to explain it in this way.

Of course, when the male Birds of Paradise (and it is the same with other birds) show off their fine plumage to the hen birds, it is because they want to marry them, which is just the same as with people; for, you know, when a gentleman wishes to marry a lady he dresses as nicely as he can, and sometimes he goes into attitudes as well. Now, the hen Birds of Paradise—so these clever people say—always choose for their husbands the birds that have the finest feathers, and the other ones, whose feathers are not so fine, have to look about for another wife. Of course, after the Birds of Paradise have married, they make a nest, and very soon there are eggs in it, and then the eggs are chipped and little Birds of Paradise come out of them. Some of these little Birds of Paradise will be males and some females, and the male ones will grow up with feathers like the cock birds, and the females with feathers like the hen—just as with us, the boys sometimes grow up like the father, and the girls sometimes grow up like the mother—only with Birds of Paradise it is always so. But now, amongst these young Birds of Paradise, though all will be beautiful, some will be more beautiful than the others, more beautiful even than their father, perhaps, and you may be sure that those will be the ones who will find it most easy to marry, and who will have the greater number of children. Some of those children will be more beautiful than *their* fathers, and then *they* will marry and have children that are still more beautiful than themselves, and so it will always be going on. The young male Birds of Paradise will always have feathers like their fathers, and gradually they will get more and more beautiful, because their wives will always choose them for their beauty. But the young female Birds of Paradise will always be like their mothers, and will not become more beautiful than they are, because hen Birds of Paradise are not chosen for their beauty, but only for their good qualities.

Now, if this is true, it shows how sensible the Birds of Paradise must be, for all *sensible* persons would choose their wives for their good qualities, and not just for their beauty. The worst of it is that there are so many *persons* who are not *quite* sensible. Still, even with us, there are a good many wives who must, I think, have been chosen, like the hen Birds of Paradise, for their good qualities—which, of course, is what they *ought* to be chosen for.

That is how some people explain why the male Birds of Paradise, and other beautiful male birds, are so much more beautiful than the females. They say that they have gradually got more and more beautiful, whilst the hens have remained plain, and that once upon a time there was not so very much difference between them. And if you ask them why the males and females of other birds are both as beautiful as each other, they will tell you that the children of *those* birds were always like the father, so that, as the father birds became beautiful—for they were chosen in the same way—all the little daughter birds became beautiful too, as well as the little sons.

But I am afraid the people who explain it all in this way must have forgotten how the Birds of Paradise, at any rate, used once to live in Paradise, where, of course, they were all as beautiful as each other, and though their plumage got spoilt when they came out of it (beautiful though it seems to us) in the way I told you, yet it does seem funny that the hens should have had it spoilt so much more than the cock birds. But you know it was spoilt by the glory which streamed out of the gates of Paradise, and which was so bright and burning that it burnt off all the most beautiful parts of it, and scorched and singed the rest. Now, of course, the nearer any bird was to the gate of Paradise when it opened, the worse he would have got scorched, and so if the cocks flew faster than the hens—and I am sure they did—they would have got soonest away, and the hens would have suffered most. *That* explanation seems much more simple; but, you see, these *clever* people do not believe about the Birds of Paradise having once lived in Paradise. They have their own explanation of it all (which I have just told you), and they like to believe in that. Then which of the two are you to believe in? Well, I think the simpler one—which is prettier as well—would be the best for you to believe in *now*, but later on—when *you* are a clever person—you can try the other. Now, you know, you are only a little child, and something that is simple and pretty is the right thing for a little child. But a clever person wants a different kind of explanation to *that*. *He* wants a clever one, and as soon as you feel that *you* have become a clever person, there will be a clever explanation all ready for you.

But now, whilst you are still a little child, I can give you another explanation of why the males and females of some birds are as beautiful as each other, whilst the males of some other ones are ever so much the most beautiful. This other explanation will do in case the one about the cock Birds of Paradise flying faster than the hens is not the right one, for, of course, we cannot be quite sure that they flew faster. I did say I was sure, but that was just a little mistake of mine. One is not *really* sure of a thing until one knows it, and I don't quite *know* that it happened like that, however much I may think it did. Besides, this new explanation that I am going to give you will do for all other birds as well as for the Birds of Paradise, and, of course, the more anything explains the better explanation it is. So now I will give it you, and, if you like it better than the other, you can take it instead, and if you only like it as well, then you will have two nice explanations instead of only one. Here it is.

In the old days, a long, long time ago, the males and females of all the birds were as beautiful as each other, and they were all in love with each other. Only the question was which of them were the most in love, and, as to that, they often had disputes. "We love you better than you love us," said the male birds to the females; "you love us only for our beauty, you do not love us for ourselves, as we love you." "If you think so," said the female birds (the beautiful hens), "give us your beauty, and you shall find that we love you just as well, without it." But the male birds, who were quite content, *really*, to be loved for their beauty, and who did not wish to part with it, made haste to change the conversation. "But *you* love *us* for *our* beauty," said the hen birds (for they soon got round again to the same subject); "it is not for ourselves that you love us, but only because we are beautiful." "If that is your idea," said the male birds, "bestow your beauty upon us, and you shall soon be undeceived." Then the female birds, who only wished to be loved for themselves and not for what they looked like, gave all their beauty to their beautiful husbands, and remained without any. So now, of course, the male birds were twice as beautiful as they had been before, whilst the poor hens were not beautiful at all, and would even have been quite ugly if they had not been birds, for a bird *cannot* be ugly. And now it was found that, whilst some of the male birds had loved their wives so much that they went on loving them still, in spite of the change in their appearance, others (and I am afraid they were the greater number) left off loving them, as soon as they had left off being beautiful, and were not able to love them again, although they tried ever so hard. You see, they had only loved them for their beauty, not for themselves, so as soon as there was no more beauty, there was no more love. So those male birds who had loved for love only, and not because their wives were beautiful, kept this beauty and added it to their own. Their wives did not want it back again, for love was enough for them. But the ones who had loved their wives, only because of their beauty, had to give it them back, for otherwise they would not have been able to go on loving them, and that would have been very awkward indeed. That is why, in some birds, the males and females are as beautiful as each other, whilst in others, the males are twice as beautiful as the females. As I told you, this is an explanation which does as well for any other bird as it does for the Birds of Paradise, and, if you like it, you can believe in it till you have grown up from a simple little child into a complicated clever person.

So now there are six Birds of Paradise that your mother has promised not to wear in her hats, not in any hat that she buys or has given to her, whether it has the whole skin of one in it, or only just a few feathers, or even one. She will not buy such a hat, and she will not go into a shop to ask the price of it. She will have nothing to do with it whatever, because she has promised.

But now, do you not see that, as your dear mother has only promised about six kinds of Birds of Paradise, and as there are some forty or fifty kinds in the world, she might easily buy a hat that had some kind of Bird of Paradise in it, without its being any of these six? How much better it would be, then, if your dear, dear mother were to promise never to wear a hat that had any kind of Bird of Paradise in it. And I am sure she will, now that you have explained to her about the wicked little demon, and how much more beautiful these Birds of Paradise are when they are alive, and how happy they are, too, and how their wives want them, to look at, and how there will be no more of them left, soon, if people keep on killing them, just to put into hats. Just talk to her about it a little, and then throw your arms round her neck and say: "Oh mother, do *promise* never to wear a hat that has the feathers of *any* Bird of Paradise in it." There! And now she has promised. Well, you see how easy it is.

# CHAPTER VII

## ABOUT HUMMING-BIRDS, AND SOME MORE EX-PLANATIONS

Perhaps, when I was telling you about the Birds of Paradise and how very, very beautiful they are, you thought they were the most beautiful birds in the whole world. They are nearly, but not quite. There are the Humming-birds—*they* are even more beautiful. At least they are more like jewels, and the Indians who live in the countries where they are found call them "living sunbeams."

"By western Indians living sunbeams named."

You can remember it by that line, which is from a poem by Mrs. Hemans, a clever lady whom your mother will tell you about. For the Indians, you know, live in America, that great country—so large that we call it "the new world"—which Columbus discovered. They do not live in India, as you might think. At least, when we talk of the Indians, it is the ones that live in America and not India that we mean. The ones that live in India we call Hindoos. It seems funny, but the reason of it is that when Columbus discovered America, he thought it was India; for it was India he had been trying to find, and he thought he had found it. But it was America, not India, and it is only in America that the beautiful Humming-birds live—birds that are so beautiful as they are want a world to themselves to live in.

Now the birds that we have been talking about—the Birds of Paradise—are not such very small birds. The largest of them is nearly as large as a crow, and even the very smallest is not so much smaller than a thrush or a starling. But the largest Humming-bird is not so large as a sparrow or chaffinch, and the smaller ones are the very smallest birds in the whole world, some of them being not so *very* much larger than a large humble-bee, which is quite wonderful to think of. Then they are wonderful fliers. The Birds of Paradise fly very well—quite well enough—but still there is nothing extraordinary in the way they fly. But the little Humming-birds dart about quite like lightning, and move their wings so fast that, when you look at them, they do not seem to be wings at all, but only two little hazy patches in the air, with a bright jewel between them, which is the gleaming breast of the Humming-bird. All the time their wings are moving so quickly, they make a humming sound, just as a top does when it is spinning very fast, which is why we call them Humming-birds, just as we call tops that hum very much, humming-tops.

We have named the Humming-birds from the sound they make when they fly, and the Indians from their bright radiance and the speed at which they dart about. It is from flower to flower that they dart, and whilst you are looking at one sunbeam that is dancing about one flower, all at once there is a ray of light through the air, and another sunbeam is dancing about another flower. That is what it looks like, only, really, it is the same sunbeam that has flown from one flower to another.

Sometimes when you are walking in the garden in England and looking at the geraniums in your flowerbeds, you will see a little brown moth hovering over one of them, and putting a long, slender thread-like thing that we call a proboscis (though we call an elephant's trunk a proboscis too) right down into the centre of the flower. *His* wings move so fast that you can hardly see them, and in a second or two *he* will dart away too, so quickly that you only know he is gone, and then, all of a sudden, you will see him again, hovering over another geranium and probing it with his wonderful, long, thin proboscis. It is a tube, that proboscis, and through it, the moth is sucking up the nectar of the flower, which is what it lives on. That moth is the humming-bird hawk-moth, and, if you have seen it, you have seen what looks more like a Humming-bird than anything else in England. It hovers over or under or in front of a flower, as the Humming-birds do, it keeps moving its wings in the same rapid way as they move theirs, and making the same humming noise with them, and it puts a long, slender, little brown thing, that looks *something* like the beak of a Humming-bird, right down into the flower, and sucks up the nectar that is in it, which is just what a Humming-bird does. So if the humming-bird moth were bright and gleaming, as Humming-birds—sunbeams—are, it would seem to be a Humming-bird and not a moth at all. But you must not think that it really would be one. Oh no, it never could be, because it is an insect, and an insect is a very different thing to a bird.

The humming-bird moth and the Humming-bird look like each other because they live in the same way and do the same things. They both fly, so they both have wings; and they both sip nectar, so they both have a long thing to stick into the flowers and suck it up with: so they look like each other, but they are not a bit the same. A petticoat, you know, looks a little like an upper skirt, for they both have to be worn round the waist, which makes them the same kind of shape, and when the skirt is part of a white dress then they are of the same colour. But think how different they really are! Why, one is a petticoat and the other is an upper skirt. So you must always remember that, though two animals look the same, they may really be very different.

Now although the Humming-birds, or living sunbeams, are all of them small birds, yet they are not all of the same size, and some are quite big compared to others, just as a peacock butterfly is quite big, compared to a tiny blue one, whilst even the tiny little blue one may be big compared to some very small moths. Then, again, their beaks are of all kinds of different shapes and lengths. Some are quite straight, whilst others are bent like a sabre or even a sickle, and one Humming-bird has his so very much bent indeed, that it looks like half of a black ring or bracelet or something else that is quite round. As for length, some are shorter than a quite short pin, whilst others are longer than a very long darning-needle.

Of course there is a reason for the beaks of Humming-birds being so different, and the reason is that they have to go into different flowers, and must fit into them as a finger fits into a fingerstall or a periwinkle into its shell. If the part of the flower that holds the nectar is straight, then the beak of the Humming-bird that feeds on the nectar of that flower must be straight too, but if it is curved, then, of course, the beak must be curved, or else how could it be pushed into it?

**RACQUET-TAILED HUMMING-BIRD**

And if the nectary of any flower (for that is what the place that the nectar is in is called) were shaped like a corkscrew, then the beak of the Humming-bird that sucked out the nectar from *that* flower would have to be shaped like a corkscrew too. But there are no flowers shaped like that, and so there are no Humming-birds with corkscrew beaks, like the tail of a periwinkle. But there *is* a flower that has its nectary, or honey-tube, bent round into almost a half circle, and it is just that one Humming-bird that has its beak bent in the same way, that sips the nectar from that flower. No other one is able to do it, and there is no other flower that that Humming-bird can sip the nectar from.

And there are more than 400 different kinds of Humming-birds, and the beak of every one of them must fit into some flower or another, and often into a great many more than one. Oh then, what a lot of different kinds of flowers there must be, for all these beaks to fit into! Ah, there are indeed, for it is in the great forests or plains of America — the largest in the whole world — or on the slopes of the great mountain ranges there — the highest in the world except the Himalayas — that the Humming-birds live, and everywhere there are wonderful trees and wonderful flowers. As for the trees, I have told you what some of them are like in the forests of the Malay Archipelago, and in the great forests of Brazil; I think they are still larger and more wonderful. And as for the flowers that grow in those wonderful forests or on the great plains or the slopes and sides of those great, high mountains, how could I ever give you an idea of what they are like, or how should I know where to begin, when there are so many? For there are some that are like great scarlet trumpets on the outside of their petals, but when you look inside them they are like the open mouths of fierce dragons shooting out a lot of fiery-or-ange tongues, all forked and cloven ever so many times over, each tongue looking as if it were the tongues of twenty little hissing snakes, all tied together in a bundle and ready to dart at you. And there are some that are in bunches, and each bunch looks as if a lot of oxen had put their heads against each other and begun to grow smaller and smaller and smaller till their horns were no longer than honeysuckles, and then had disappeared altogether, *except* their horns, which had turned pink and stayed there. Bunches of little pink ox-horns are what those flowers look like. Then there are flowers that look as if they had almost changed into very beautiful butterflies, and others that seem to be very beautiful butterflies just changing into flowers. There are flowers that are all the colours that there are, and others that have tried all the colours that there are, and then found out new ones to be of. And there are some, too, that are only white, but so lovely that all the flowers of all the colours that there are, gaze at them and envy them. Some are so soft and delicate that, although you see them, you only seem to be dreaming of them. They make you think of heaven, and it is as if angels were kissing you. Others are like golden stars, with a stem that is like a long, long, very long piece of red string that goes ty-ing itself round and round a great many trees, and climbing up and up them, and all the way up there are bright green leaves and the beautiful golden stars. Other strings are golden or green, and have pink or crimson stars upon them, and some of these hang down, like glowing lamps from a soft, cool, emerald ceiling. Some flowers are like little bunches of red counters that you play games with, and there is one that is like a wonderful, scarlet, shining leaf, with a thick little tail at the tip of it, twisted round in a coil. This tail is orange with cream-white spots upon it, but just at its *own* tip it is scarlet again, like the rest of the leaf. Such a wonderful-look-ing flower! There are creeping crimson nasturtiums that make the air blush in spots, azaleas with scarlet that has swooned into pink, and pink that has blushed into scarlet, and calceolarias that look like yellow flower-bubbles that fairies have blown into the air and that have come down, softly, upon delicate little stalks, and stayed there without bursting. Not all of these wonderful flowers have a scent, for scented flowers are commoner here in England than in far-off tropical countries. But a few of them have, and *their* scent is so exquisite that you would think it was sent from heaven.

Some of the flowers have leaves that are even more beautiful than themselves, and sometimes it is the leaves that you look at and not the flowers at all. Some of these leaves seem to be made of velvet, or something even softer and more velvety *than* velvet, whilst the colours in them are like the pattern of a very beautiful Turkey carpet. Others look like wonderful spear-heads or the tops of very ornamental park railings, green and red and orange, and all striped and spotted and speckled like the skin of newts or lizards. There are some leaves so large, too, that they would almost make a carpet for a *very* small room, and so handsome that you might go into all the haberdashers' shops in the world without finding any carpet that would look nearly so well. Some are still larger, and those are the leaves of palm-trees that bend down from high in the air, at the end of long, bending stalks that spring from the top of the small slender stem. They are of such a soft, lovely green that it makes you cool even to look up at them, and so graceful and delicate that you think of the fairies, but so big and strong that a giant might lie upon them and go to sleep, without breaking them or crushing them down. And there are wonderful cactuses—so large that they are called trees—with trunks like great, prickly, green caterpillars, and branches like smaller, prickly, green caterpillars stuck on to them by the tail. But on these ugly branches there are flowers like beautiful purple stars, whilst in the pools or the rivers, water-lilies are floating that look like large, purple flakes of snow. It is amongst flowers and leaves and trees like these that the Humming-birds fly about. Those are the wonderful goblets out of which they sip their nectar.

But now, about this sipping of nectar I have something to tell you, and when I have told it you, you will know more than a good many people do, who think they know something about Humming-birds and natural history. Well, it is this: the Humming-birds do not live *only* on the nectar in the flowers, as most people think they do, but on the insects that have been drowned in it, and which they suck up at the same time. You see the insects—of course I mean little insects—flies or gnats, not large moths and butterflies—get into the tubes of the flowers, to sip the nectar themselves, and they often fall into it, and are not able to get out again, but drown there; for to them it is like a little lake or pond—a pond of nectar, and, of course, very nice, but still, for all that, it drowns them. There is hardly any flower-cup that has not these drowned insects in it, and when the Humming-birds drink the nectar, they swallow the little insects at the same time. They could not live upon nectar only—they want animal food (as it is called) as well, and that is the way in which they get it. That is why when people have caught Humming-birds, and given them only nectar—or sugar and water, which is something like it—to live on, they have always died. There are no insects in it, no animal food. They had gravy, you see, but no meat, and they wanted meat as well as gravy. So they died, the poor Humming-birds. But I think it is almost better for a living sunbeam to die than to be kept living in a cage.

But now, why do the Indians call the Humming-birds living sunbeams? Oh, but you will say I have told you that, and, besides, anybody could guess. It is because they are so bright and gleaming, and hover in the air as a sunbeam dances in it, or shoot through it as quickly and as brightly as a sunbeam shoots down from the sun. Well, yes, that is one explanation; but why should there not be two (as there were about the Birds of Paradise), so that you can choose the one you like best?—for you know you are not a clever person *yet*. Well, there *are* two, for the Indians say that the Humming-birds are called living sunbeams because they really *are* living sunbeams, just as you are called a little girl because you are a little girl; and how could there be a simpler explanation of a thing than that?

And this is how it happened, only you must remember that it was a very, very long time ago. In those old days the sun had not long sent his beams to earth, and it was only after they came there that the things upon the earth began to live. There had been no life at all before, it had all been dark and cold; it was only when the sun's beams began to shine upon the cold, dark earth, that they warmed it into life and love. Now as first one beautiful thing and then another began to live upon the earth, the sunbeams admired them all very much, but they did not envy them, for there was nothing there *quite* so beautiful as a sunbeam. But one day, as they were dancing upon the waters of the sea, they heard the fishes saying to each other: "How beautiful are the sunbeams! Is there anything so beautiful as they? Our scales flash out brightly, but compared to them they are dull, even on the sunniest day. We should envy them, were they alive like us, but of course, as it is, it is different." "Are we not alive?" said the sunbeams, and they felt sad and did not dance on the waves any more that day. Then, another day, they were dancing on the leaves, and falling through them on to the shady ground underneath, chequering it with gold. "How glorious are the sunbeams!" said the leaves to each other, "more glorious even than the birds or the butterflies that perch amongst us. Would that we were as beautiful!" "Do you envy them?" said a butterfly, who had overheard and felt annoyed; "they have neither sense nor breath, are neither born nor die. Envy us, if you will, who have all these advantages, and are so beautiful as well—much more so than yourselves—but do not, however plain you may be, envy what is not alive." "Are we not alive?" said the sunbeams, and they were discontented and the clouds hid them, so that neither the trees nor the birds and butterflies within them seemed to be alive any more. And, again, the sunbeams were shining through a small window, where, in a wretched garret, on a still more wretched bed, lay a man who had care and sorrow—yes, and worse even than those—in his heart. "Would that I were dead!" he cried, as he clasped his hands on his forehead. "Ah, how I envy the sunbeams! But no, I will not envy *them*, for *they* are not alive, they are inanimate merely." "Are we not alive?" said the sunbeams; "and does nobody envy us on that account?" And the wretched room that had seemed quite cheerful whilst they were there, became dark and dismal again, as they withdrew.

And now it was the sunbeams who envied everything—bird or beast, or plant or leaf or flower (even the man in the garret)—because they were alive. "It is hard that we alone should be without life," thought they, and they complained to the sun. "Give us life," they cried; "we are more beautiful than anything here on earth, but nothing envies us because we are not alive. It is dreadful not to be envied." "And do you really think," said the sun, "that you, who have given life to others, have no life yourselves? Before I sent you to the earth, it was dark and cold and lifeless. It needed you, to give it that for which you now ask. Do not, then, be discontented any more, but be assured that you have life, as much as anything that lives and grows upon the earth, though, to be sure, it is of another kind. Be satisfied, therefore, and rejoice in your loveliness." This answer of the sun's satisfied most of the sunbeams, but there were some who were foolish and whom it did not satisfy. "Give us such life as the children of the earth enjoy!" cried these; "the life that breathes and grows, that has a shape, that is born and dies. That is the life that we would have. Be good to us, and give us that." Then the sun said to the foolish sunbeams: "I can give you such life as you ask for, and, if you persist in asking it, I must; for you are my children and I cannot bear to see you unhappy. But remember, if I once grant you this wish, and give you the life that earth's children enjoy, you can nevermore be as you now are, or enter into my palace—my golden palace—again. Now you fly from me to the earth and from the earth back to me, but when once you have earth's life, on earth you must remain and on earth you must die. You are immortal now: when you become children of the earth you will be mortal as they are."

But the foolish sunbeams, who could not understand what death should be, persisted, and the sun, who loved them because they were his children, had to do what they asked. So one night, when all the other sunbeams had flown back to him, he sent these foolish ones to sleep on the earth (which had never happened to them before), and there they lay all night—some in the flower-cups, some under the leaves of the trees—without giving any light at all, for when a sunbeam *is* asleep it can give no light. But in the morning, when their brother and sister sunbeams flew back to earth, they woke up, but the two did not know each other again, for the foolish sunbeams were not sunbeams any more—not real ones, that is to say. They flew about, still, in the forests, and glanced through the trees, and hovered over the flowers, in almost the same way as they had done before; but now they had a shape and wings, and they sipped the nectar out of the flower-cups, which was a thing that they had never even dreamed about. They were Humming-birds, and though their feathers were as bright as *they* had ever been, and though they had all of them long Latin names and a scientific description in books, still it was not quite the same, for it would take a lot of Latin and a lot of scientific description, to make up for not being a sunbeam. But when the Indians came to know of the occurrence, they called them "living sunbeams," and it is easy to understand what they meant. And now you know (until you are a clever person) how Humming-birds came into the world. But you must not think that the other sunbeams—the real ones that have never changed into anything—are dead. Oh no, indeed! How could they dance and play about as they do, if they were?

PLOVER CREST HUMMING-BIRD

# CHAPTER VIII

## SOME VERY BRIGHT HUMMING-BIRDS

One of the most beautiful of all the Humming-birds (but we can say that of so many) is the Rainbow Humming-bird. It is very large for a Humming-bird, so what *will* you think when I say that its body is about the size of a little wren's, a bird which, perhaps, you had been thinking was the smallest bird there is. Why, a Humming-bird that is as big, or almost as big, as a wren is a very big Humming-bird indeed—in fact quite a gigantic one. But now, the tail of this Humming-bird is very different to a wren's, and makes it look still bigger because it is so long—three to three and a half inches, I should think—and such a wonderful shape. It is forked, so you must think of a swallow first if you want to imagine it; but then you must imagine that the two feathers which make the fork of a swallow's tail are curved outwards like two little scimitars, so that their tips are six inches apart from each other. Indeed they gleam as brightly as any scimitar does in the sun, but it is not like steel that they gleam, for they are of the most lovely deep, rich, violet-blue that you can imagine, such a colour as was never seen anywhere else out of the rainbow; and now I come to think of it, what these lovely feathers are most like is two little violet rainbows set back to back. You can think how lovely they look as they go darting through the air, and I must tell you that the beautiful violet-blue sends out gleams of other kinds of blues—lighter ones—which are just as beautiful as the violet itself. On the opposite page you see the picture of a Humming-bird that is a good deal like this one. But it is not the same, so the tail is not *quite* the same either.

Now of course you will think—and you will be quite right to think so—that a bird that has a tail like two little violet rainbows will have the other parts of him beautiful as well. Well, the back of this bird is all green—a beautiful, shining, gleaming green, and his head is green too—at least it seems to be when you see it first; but, as you look at it, all at once the green changes into a heavenly violet blue, to match the heavenly violet blue of its lovely rainbow tail. Under the throat it is green like the rest, but just in the centre of it there is a tiny little drop—just one or two little feathers—of the very loveliest amethyst. Ah, fancy seeing a bird like that flying about and hovering over the flowers. Only you would not *see* him, for you would not be able to see his wings—at least not properly—they would move so fast. What you would see, would be a little circle of hazy brown mist, and, right in the middle of it, a little sparkling sun, and on the other side, gleaming through the mist, two sweet little violet rainbows. Then all at once there would be a trail of light in the air, and it would all be somewhere else—another sun and rainbows over another flower. Of course, really, a Humming-bird would have flown from one flower to another, but what it would look like would be a gleam of light—a sunbeam—with a jewel-flash at each end of it.

**TRAIN-BEARER HUMMING-BIRD**

Another Humming-bird—the Sappho Comet—is about the same size as the last one, and he is a lovely gleaming green, too—an emerald green, I think—on his head and neck and shoulders, but his throat is light blue—the colour of a most beautiful turquoise. But *such* a turquoise! There is no other one in the world that ever gleamed and flashed and sparkled in that way, because, you know, turquoises do not sparkle at all—at least nowhere else—it is not their habit. But I think that some of the very finest of them—at least the lovely colours that were in them—must have flown into that Humming-bird's throat and begun to gleam and flash and sparkle there. Perhaps they begged to be allowed to as a very special favour. Then the tail of this Humming-bird is forked too, like the other one's, but not in quite the same way. It is more like the fork of an arrow than two little rainbows turned back to back, and instead of being violet it is all ruby and copper and topaz, with a broad band of velvet black at each tip. I cannot tell you how brilliant those colours are—the ruby and the copper and the topaz. They are so brilliant that, if you were to take them into a dark room, I really almost think they would light it up like a lamp or a candle. Oh, it is a wonderful tail. You might think and think for quite a long time and yet you would never be able to think how bright—how wonderfully bright—it is.

But listen to what the Indians say. They say that once that Humming-bird was out in a thunderstorm, and the lightning got angry with him because he flew so fast, and tried to strike him. It was jealous of him, that was the reason, for the lightning likes to think itself faster than anything else. But although the lightning chased that Humming-bird for a very long time, it could only just touch his tail, and there it has stayed—a little flash of it which was not enough to hurt—ever since. You know how bright the lightning is; that will help you to think what that Humming-bird's tail is like. And you know, now, what his throat is like. Fancy seeing them both together, flashing, sparkling, gleaming, beaming, glancing, dancing in the glorious, glowing sunshine of South America.

But now in the Splendid-breasted Humming-bird all the glory is upon his breast, his throat. Once, I think (at least the Indians say so), he must have flown very high—yes, right up to heaven, and the door was open and he tried to fly in. But he could not, they turned him away; but the glory of heaven had just fallen upon his breast and he flew back with it there, to earth. It is green—that glory—the most marvellous, light, gleaming green, but all at once, as you look at it, it has changed to blue, an exquisite light, turquoise blue, and then, just as you are going to cry out, "Oh, but it is blue, not green," it is green again, and then blue again before you can say that it is green, and then, all at once, it is both at the same time, for each has changed into the other.

It is the throat-gorget (you know I explained to you) on which this glorious colour falls, but this bird has such a large one that it covers the breast as well as the throat, and goes up quite high on each side, till it meets the deep, rich, velvety black of the head. Of course this deep, velvet black makes the wonderful green and blue look all the more wonderful, for it is a dark background for them to shine out against, and your mother will explain to you what a background is. Then, on the back this Humming-bird is green too—in fact you might call him the emerald Humming-bird—but it is darker than that other green (if anything so bright *can* be darker) and without the lovely turquoise-blue in it. It is a glory, but not *such* a glory as the one on his breast; not the glory of heaven that fell upon him at its gates—perhaps it is his memory of it as he flew away.

But now I feel sure you will ask why the same brightness which streamed out of heaven, and spoilt the plumage of the Birds of Paradise, should have made the plumage of this Humming-bird so beautiful. Well, it is a difficult question, but perhaps it is because the Humming-bird was thinking of heaven, and wishing to get into it, whilst the Birds of Paradise had got tired of being in heaven and were only thinking of earth. That might have made a very great difference. And *perhaps* you will say, "If the Humming-birds are sunbeams that have been changed into birds, why should some of them have been made more beautiful afterwards in other ways?" Well, as to that, there are a great many different kinds of Humming-birds (more than four hundred, as I told you), so perhaps they were not quite all of them sunbeams first, and besides, even when a bird has been a sunbeam first, something else might happen to it when it had become a bird. At any rate, if one explanation does not seem satisfactory, there is always the other, and one of them must be the right one—until you are a clever person, which will not be yet awhile. So now we will go on, for there are some other Humming-birds with other explanations waiting.

The Glow-glow Humming-bird (I do like that name) is smaller than any of the other three we have talked about, for it is less than half the size of a little wren. Its head and its back are shining green (you will be thinking all the Humming-birds are green, but wait a little!), its breast is white, but its throat—oh, its throat!—what is it? What can it be called? It is a rose that has burst into flame. No, it is a flame trying to look like a rose. No, it is neither of these. It is one of those stars that are of all colours, and change from one to the other as you look at them—from green to gold, from gold to topaz, from topaz to rosy red. Only *this* star changed into every colour at once, which was wonderful, and as he did that (and this was still more wonderful) he flew all to pieces, and little bits of him were scattered through the whole air, and when the sun rose and shone upon them, they were all Humming-birds, flying about with wings and feathers, and with long Latin names, so that there should be no doubt about it. It was wonderful, wonderful; but yet it was not quite so wonderful as the colours upon this Humming-bird's throat.

The Little Flame-bearer (there is a name for you!) is a still smaller Humming-bird than the last one—indeed his body, without the feathers, would not be *very* much larger than a *very* large humble-bee. Here, again, all the wonder is on its throat, which is topaz and green and copper, all glowing and sparkling together, as if they were all married to one another and each of them was trying to get the upper hand. Ah, was there ever such a sweet little gem-bird? He is a jewel mounted on wings and set in the air. Only sometimes, when he hovers just underneath a flower, he seems hanging from its tip like a pendant.

Costa's Coquette (that means that some one named Costa—some Portuguese gentleman—was the first to write about it) is larger than the Little Flame-bearer (though not half so big as a wren), and he *tries* to be brighter. Whether he *is* brighter I am sure I can't say. To tell properly, one ought to see them both hovering under the same flower, or, at least, very close together, and even then one would only feel bewildered. But this one's head and throat are all one splendour, one marvellous gleam of rosy, pinky, rosy-pink, pinky-rose magenta. Only if you *say* that that is what it is, it will change into violet and contradict you, and then, if you say it is violet, it will change into topaz and contradict you again. So you had better say nothing—for one does not want to be contradicted—but just hold your breath and watch it. It will change quite soon enough, even then, long before you are tired of its rosy, pinky, rosy-pink, pinky-rose magenta, which is a colour you have not seen, and which I have not told you about before. Only if you *must* say something about it whilst you are looking at it—something besides "Oh!" I mean—say it is a Humming-bird. That will be quite sufficient, and not one of its colours can be offended with you then for not mentioning them and mentioning the others. Now, I must tell you that the feathers of this little bird's throat—of that wonderful, gleaming throat-gorget—grow out on each side into two little peaks, two little pointed tongues of rose-pink magenta flame (but hush!), and he can spread them out and shoot them forward, as well as the whole of the gorget, in quite a wonderful way. When he does that, what he *seems* to do is to strike a great number of matches at the same time, and from each one, as he strikes it, there bursts out hundreds and hundreds of bright, sparkling jewels of flame. Ah, you should see him strike his jewel-matches—all together, all the jewels that there are, all struck in one second, as he whizzes about in the air. His back is all green, and *so* bright, if only you cover up his head and throat. If you don't cover them—or as soon as you uncover them again—you hardly seem to see it. It is no brighter then than a glow-worm is when a very bright star is shooting through the air.

Now we come to the Splendid Coquette, a little bird not half the size of a golden-crested wren, which is the smallest bird that we, in this country, know anything about, smaller, even, than the common wren. *He* has a crest, too—this little Humming-bird—a very fine one of chestnut feathers, not sticking up on the top of the head, as so many crests do, but going backwards after the head has come to an end, so that it makes a little chestnut feather-awning for the neck to be under. But just where they spring from the head each of these chestnut feathers is black, and at their tips, too, they have all a little black spot, and this makes them look still prettier than if they were all chestnut. When the little bird spreads out this fine crest of his, like a fan—for he can do that—all the feathers in it stand out separately from each other, and then he looks like a little sun in the centre of his own rays.

Yes, a sun, because he is so very bright. He has a gorget (or perhaps you would prefer to call it a lappet) of feathers on his throat and breast, of the most glorious, radiant green colour, and from it there shoot out—one on each side—a pair of the very loveliest and most delicate little fairy-wings that ever you *never* saw—for I feel sure that you never *have* seen anything at all like them. I do not mean, of course, that they are real wings, to fly with, no—it would be funny if a bird had *two* pairs of *that* kind—but ornamental ones, wings for the little hen Humming-bird, who has none, to look at and say, "How beautiful! How *extraordinarily* becoming!" Each of these dear little wings is made by a few delicate, long, slender feathers of a light chestnut colour, the same as the feathers of the crest, only, instead of being tipped with black, these ones are tipped with a spot of the same lovely green that there is on the throat and breast. The longest of them, which is in the middle, is nearly an inch long—which is very long indeed when you think how small the little birdie is—and it stands out a quarter of an inch beyond the two next longest ones on each side of it, and these are almost a quarter of an inch longer than the ones that come next. If you hold out your hand with the fingers spread out, and imagine the middle one a good deal longer and the little finger and thumb much shorter, then you will know the shape of these dear little fairy-wings; only, of course, feathers are much more elegant than fingers—even than pretty little fingers. Think how pretty something in muslin or puff-lace, like that, on a dress would be!—but it is ever, oh, *ever* so much prettier on a little Humming-bird, in little chestnut feathers with little green spangles at their tips. And that is why I call them "fairy-wings," for I think if any pair of wings that are *not* a fairy's could be pretty enough *for* a fairy, those would be the ones.

And I think if you saw this sweet little Humming-bird hanging in the air, with his breast all flashing and sparkling, and with his chestnut crest spread out above it, and his little chestnut and star-spangled wings flying out on each side of it, you would think him almost as pretty as a fairy could be. You would think his fairy-wings the real ones that he was flying with, because you would see them, whilst the other ones would be moving so quickly that they would be only like a mist or haze—a little night that he had made for himself for the star of his beauty to shine in.

Now just try to imagine how lovely that little Humming-bird must be. Can you understand any one *wanting* to kill him? But now that I have told you about that wretched little demon with his charms to send people to sleep, and those two bad bottles of his, or, rather, the powders inside them—apathy and vanity—I daresay you can understand it. If I had not told you about *him* I don't think you would have been able to.

Princess Helen's Coquette (how proud he ought to be of a name like that!) is a little Humming-bird something like the last one. He is a little smaller, I think, but whether he is a little prettier, too, or not *quite* so pretty, or only *as* pretty, all that I shall leave to you; it is you who will have to decide. His back is all of a golden green, and his head, which has a forked crest at the back of it like a swallow's tail, is a beautiful, rich, dark, velvety green, so that would make a pretty little bird— would it not?—even without anything else. But he *has* something else—two or three other things in fact—which are so—oh, so *very* pretty. First, on each side of the back of the head—just under each fork of the little swallow-tailed crest—there is a little delicate tuft of feathers, which rise up and spread out upon each side in such a graceful little curve. But these feathers are not like other feathers. They are *something* like the "funny feathers" that the Birds of Paradise have, for they are quite thin, like threads, and an inch long, which (although it is not quite so long as those) is yet a good length when you think of what a little thing this little Humming-bird is. These pretty little feathers are of a deep velvety green colour—the same colour as his swallow-tailed crest—and there are three on each side, three little velvet green feather-threads, floating out on each side behind his head. On his throat there is a gorget of gleaming, jewelly green, much lighter than the other greens—more like emerald, but with a goldeny, bronzy wash in it, as well. Just think how beautiful that must be! And then, lower down on his throat, underneath the green gorget—as if all that were not enough for him—this Humming-bird has something else—we will call it a tippet—which flies out all round his neck, and, especially, on each side of it. A tippet or a ruffle—perhaps that is rather a better word—a ruffle of velvet black feathers in front, and of light chestnut feathers with velvet black stripes—like a tiger—on each side. As for his tail, it spreads out into a dear little fan, and the fan is chestnut and black too, broad stripes of chestnut and narrow stripes of black, with a broad patch of black where it begins, which looks like the handle of the fan. What a pretty, pretty bird! Fancy a little birdie that is only about two inches long, and has a crest like a swallow-tail on his head, a gorget—or lappet—on his throat, a tippet—or ruffle—just underneath the gorget, and a little spray of feather-threads on each side of his head, just underneath the crest! Fancy killing such a little fairy-bird as that! Fancy *wanting* to kill him! But it is all the little demon. It is he who has blown about his nasty powders and frozen the hearts of the *poor* women, who are *really* so kind—at any rate they *would* be if only he would let them.

Did I say, "Such a little fairy-bird"? I think I did, and I was quite right, for it is just this very little Humming-bird that the fairies are so fond of riding on. They go two at a time, sometimes. One sits on his back, and another lies on the broad fan of his tail, and the one on the back uses the little feather-threads as reins. It is so grand! The Humming-bird dashes up at the fairy's own flower-door, and hovers there till she is ready to come out, and then dashes away with her to another flower, where another fairy lives. And that is how the fairies call upon each other in countries where there are Humming-birds. Perhaps you will think that a Humming-bird—even quite a little Humming-bird (and they are none of them big)—is *rather* a large gee-gee for a *fairy* to ride on. But you must remember that in tropical countries fairies grow to quite a remarkable size.

Well, that is eight Humming-birds that I have tried to describe to you (though it is very like trying to describe a sunset to some one who has never seen one), and perhaps you think I have chosen all the most beautiful ones first, and that there are no more left which are *quite* so pretty. But I think I can find just one more that is not such a *very* plain bird, not a bird you would call ugly if you were to see it hovering about over a bed of geraniums or under a cluster of honeysuckle, some bright spring or summer morning when you happened to go out into your garden. So we will take that one, and, if he is not pretty enough, you must just try to put up with him.

He is called the Sun Beauty. Perhaps you would think him dark at first, for his head and back and shoulders are of such a rich, deep, velvety green that it almost goes into black velvet—all except one little spot on the forehead, just above the beak, and that never can look *quite* black. Sometimes it does *almost*, just for one second, but the next second it flashes into green again, and oh, how it gleams and sparkles and throws out little jewels, little splashes of sun-fire all round it! What a wonderful green it is!—at first, and then—oh, what a wonderful—but really there is no proper name for *that* colour. I was going to say "blue," and perhaps it is more like blue than anything else, but nothing else is quite like it. Then, just at the beginning of this Humming-bird's throat—just under the chin—there are a few feathers that are like a kind of dusky-smoked-magenta-bronze-jewelry, and a little farther down they gleam into ruddy bronze and coppery topaz, and then—oh, what *is* that? The very sun himself has flashed out from his throat, from his gorget—yes, a little flake of the sun, a sunflake instead of a snowflake. Oh, it is *such* a gorget, a gorget of golden topaz, of coppery gold, of green gold, of silver gold, of silver, of gleaming white, of all these together, and it spreads out on each side like a wonderful fan, and shoots out in front of all the other feathers. Such a gorget! The feathers in it are not feathers at all—I do not think they *can* be feathers—they are sunflakes, as I have told you.

That is what this Humming-bird is like on the throat. Underneath the throat, on the breast, he becomes green again, not the dark velvet green of the back, but a still more glorious green, gleaming and brilliant, but soft and rich at the same time. It is a green that changes, too—changes almost into blue. I will tell you how that is. Once this green—this wonderful, lovely green—did not think itself lovely enough (which was funny), so it said to the blue of the violet and the turquoise and the amethyst and the sapphire: "Come and make part of me, but I must be the greater part." "That is not fair," cried the blues of all those lovely things; "we will come, since you have invited us, but we intend to have the upper hand." "Come then," said the green, "and let us fight for the mastery. Whichever wins, the other will be improved by it. We will struggle together, and we will see which is the strongest." So they came, those blues of wonder, from the violet, the turquoise, the sapphire, and the amethyst—yes, and from the sky, the stars, and the sea as well—and they fell in a glory on that glorious green that had been there before them, and fought with it to possess the breast of that Humming-bird. And they are fighting to possess it now. They gleam and flash and sparkle and glow, and try to out-glory each other; but I think that that wonderful green is the strongest, although he has such a lot of blues to fight against. But stronger than any and than all of them is the sun on that Humming-bird's gorget, that gorget of gold and topaz, and copper and bronze, and silver and gleaming white.

That is what that Humming-bird is like, and that is how he got some of his wonderful colours; so, at least, the Indians say, only some of them say that it was the blues who were there first, and asked the green to come. But always, in history, you will find that there are different opinions about the same thing. People are not *all* agreed, even about the battle of Waterloo.

So, you see, we have been able to find one other handsome Humming-bird, at any rate. And then there is the Hermit Humming-bird. I must just describe him. His head and neck are—brown, the whole of his back is—brown, his wings, his throat, and his breast are—brown, and all the rest of him is—brown. Why, then, he is all brown, without any colours at all, unless there are some lying asleep, and ready to wake up and dart out all of a sudden, in the way I have explained to you. No, there are no colours, either asleep or awake, or, at any rate, hardly any. Compared to the Humming-birds I have been telling you about, this one is just a plain, dull bird, as plain and as dull, almost, as his wife, for that, you know, is what the wives of Humming-birds are like. Then is he a Humming-bird at all? Surely he is not one; he must be some other bird. Oh no, he is not. He is a Humming-bird, but he is a Hermit Humming-bird. I have not told you before—but now I will tell you—that there are some Humming-birds—in fact a good many—that have no bright colours at all, and *they* are called hermits. A hermit, you know, is a person who lives in a cell or cave, and wears a long, brown gown, with a hood at one end of it for his head, and never dresses gaily or goes out to see things, but has what *we* should consider a very dull life; only as *he* likes it that makes it all right—for *him*. So these dull-coloured Humming-birds are called hermits, not because they live in cells, because, of course, they do not, but because they have no bright things to wear, but only brown gowns, like hermits. But now as Humming-birds used once to be sunbeams, and are still *living* sunbeams that have been changed into birds, how does it happen that any of them have become hermits, with nothing showy about them? That is a thing which requires an explanation, so it is lucky that there is one all ready for it in the next chapter. Not all the things that require an explanation are so lucky as that. Some of them go on requiring one all their lives, and yet never get what they require. I have known several of that sort.

# CHAPTER IX

## HERMIT HUMMING-BIRDS AND TWO OTHER ONES

I told you that as soon as the sun's light fell upon the earth all the sunbeams that had been asleep there woke up, and were changed into Humming-birds. But there was just one sunbeam who had gone to sleep in a cave, and when *he* woke up it was quite dark, and so *he* was changed into a Humming-bird without any colours, and when his brother Humming-birds saw him they laughed at him, and called him a hermit. It was very wrong of them to do so, for it was not his fault that he was brown. There is nothing wrong in going to sleep in a cave, and, of course, he could not tell what would happen. But they thought he looked ridiculous, coming out of it all brown, like a hermit. I don't think that made him ridiculous, really, but, even if it did, they should not have laughed at him. We should not laugh at people because they are ridiculous. It makes them unhappy, and, besides, we may be sure that in some way or other we are just as ridiculous as they are, *We* may not know in what way. *That* only shows how ignorant we are. It is best not to laugh at other people. If we *want* to laugh at any one, we can always laugh at ourselves.

Now, this poor Hermit Humming-bird was unhappy because he alone had no colours, and because all the other Humming-birds laughed at him. He complained of it to the sun, who was his father, and explained how it had happened. "It is unfortunate," said the sun; "but since I was unable to shine upon you, when you awoke, I cannot give you my own livery to wear now. But do not be unhappy. The world is full of brightness and beauty, and if you go about asking for some of it from those who have it, none of them will refuse you, when they know that you are one of my children. They will grant it you for the love of me, for I am loved of all that live upon the earth. In this way, though I cannot clothe you directly from myself, it will come to the same thing in the end, for it is through me that all things have their beauty, so that in having what was theirs you will have what is mine, and still you will be a living sunbeam. Only do not ask any of your brother Humming-birds to give you anything, because then you will not be under an obligation to them." (Your mother will explain to you what being under an obligation is, and how very many *you* are under to *her*.)

So the poor Hermit Humming-bird went about through the world, asking all the beautiful things in it for some of their beauty, and not one that he asked refused him, for the love of his father the sun. He begged of the clouds at sunset, when they were all crimson lake, and at sunrise, when they were all topaz and amber, and all three of these lovely colours fell upon his throat and struggled for the mastery, like the green and blue on the breast of that other Humming-bird that I have told you about. Then he begged of the bluest stars in the sky, and just on the outer edge of his now lovely throat, on the edge of that shining gorget, there fell such a blue as made one feel in heaven only to look at it. After that he begged of the sea that the sun was shining on in the morning, and now his head was of the loveliest pale sea-green, and then, again, he begged of it a little later in the day, and his back became a darker green, almost, if not quite, as lovely as the lovely one on his head. Thus he went about the world, begging and asking, and he did not forget either the jewels, or the flowers, or the colours that live in the rainbow. And at the end of the day this Humming-bird that had been all brown, and that his brothers had called a hermit, was one of the loveliest of all the Humming-birds, and his English name (we won't trouble about the Latin one) was the All-glorious Humming-Bird. He was not called a hermit any more, after that, but those Humming-birds that had called him one, and laughed at him when he was brown, were changed into hermits themselves. That is how there came to be Hermit Humming-birds in the world, and one of them is the one that surprised you so much when I described him to you, because he was all brown. They are all of them brown, but you must not laugh at them, for all that, even though they did at their brother. They have their punishment, and it is bad enough to be punished and made all brown, without being laughed at about it as well.

Now, of course, as all the Hermit Humming-birds are brown, it would be no use to describe them to you, one at a time, like the others. Instead of that I will tell you about some more Humming-birds who are pretty, and who came to be what they are like now in some curious way or other, which had nothing to do with their having once been sunbeams. One of these is the Snow-cap. He is very small, almost as small as the smallest of the Humming-birds—and you know how small that is—and although he is not exactly brown, still he is not at all a brilliant bird for a Humming-bird. What makes him so pretty is this. First, all the whole crown of his head is of a beautiful, pure, silky white, which makes it look as if a large, soft snowflake had fallen upon it, and then, when he spreads out his tail like a fan—which you may be sure he knows how to do—there are two white patches upon it as well, which look like two smaller snowflakes. It is not many Humming-birds who are ornamented in *that* way. How did this one get those white patches, and are they really snowflakes that fell upon him? You shall hear. Once they were not white at all, those patches, but coloured with all the colours of the rainbow, and more brilliant than anything you could possibly think of, more brilliant even than any other colour that is upon any other Humming-bird. Indeed they were *so* brilliant that no one could look at them, and that made the Humming-bird very proud indeed. "Could my rivals have looked at me," he said, "they would never have confessed my superiority, however plainly they must have seen it. Not to be able to look at me is, in itself, a confession. They are dazzled, and well they may be, for to look at me is like looking at the sun himself. Surely there is no earthly brightness that I do not outshine." And as the proud bird said this, he looked up, and there, far above him in the blue dome of the sky, were the snows of the mighty mountain Chimborazo, and in their white, dazzling purity they seemed even brighter than himself. But instead of being humbled, the Humming-bird only felt insulted, and resolved to do something decisive. "I will thaw those white robes of his," he said; "my brightness shall burn them away, and there shall be no more snow in the world." He was just a little larger than a humble-bee.

So up this Humming-bird flew, right on to the top of Chimborazo, the great high mountain, where there was snow everywhere. "Have you come to thaw me?" said the snow, as it fell around him. "That is ridiculous. We shall see which of us is best able to extinguish the other." With that one snowflake fell upon his head and two more upon his tail, just over those three patches that had been so marvellously bright. He tried to shake them off, but he could not. They stayed there, and instead of having been able to thaw them, it was *they* who had put *his* brightness quite out. All those wonderful colours were gone now, and there was only the snow-white. "Fly back," said the snow, "or I will quite cover you. You have lost that of which you were so proud, but you have me in exchange. Fly back, and be a wiser bird for the future." So the Humming-bird flew back, ashamed and crestfallen, and fearing to show himself. "What will the others say when they see me?" he thought. But when the other Humming-birds saw him, they all cried out, "Oh, look! What beautiful bird is this that has come to dwell amongst us? What an exquisite white! Surely he has been to the top of Chimborazo and brought down some of its snow upon him. How pure and how lovely!" Yes, they could look at him now, and they thought him more beautiful than when they were blinded and dazzled. That is how that Humming-bird got his snow-white patches. He had no colours now with which to outrival the other Humming-birds, but he could put up with that, for the white snow was lovelier than them all.

And then there is the Humming-bird that the Indians call the Jewel-flower-sunrise-and-sunset-Humming-bird (only they have one word for it, which makes it sound better). I have forgotten what his English name is—I am not quite sure if he has one. This Humming-bird was very beautiful to begin with, so beautiful, indeed, that the flowers, as he hovered over them, fell in love with him and wished to give him their colours to wear, for their sakes. But the Humming-bird did not want their colours, for he thought his own were much more beautiful. "If you sparkled like jewels," he said, "as well as being soft and bright, then it would be different. But your beauty is too homely. You are not sufficiently refulgent." (That was a word he was fond of, for he had heard it applied to himself. Your mother will tell you what it means).

So the flowers prayed to the sun from whom they have their beautiful colours, and the sun made them like jewels—jewels of the rose and the violet, of the lily and the daffodil, the sunflower, the pink and carnation. Perhaps they were not just the same flowers as those, for they grew in America, but they had all their colours and many more. "That is an improvement certainly," said the Humming-bird, when he had looked at them. "You are much more beautiful now, but you remain the same all day long. It is very different with the sky. Every morning and evening when the sun rises and sets, she has quite a special beauty, and it is only then that she can be said to be refulgent. If it were so with you, then I might take you, but I do not care for flowers who have no sunrise or sunset." So the flowers prayed to the sun again, and he made them as much more beautiful when he rose and set at morning and evening as the sky is then in the east and west. And when the Humming-bird saw that they were really refulgent, he took all their colours, and, for a little while, the flowers were quite pale, and only got bright again by degrees. But they never flashed and sparkled like jewels any more, and there was never another flower sunrise or another flower sunset. The Humming-bird kept all that for himself; he never gave any of it back to the flowers. It was not very generous of him. I *think* he was going to be punished for it, but, somehow or other, it was forgotten. Punishments do get forgotten, sometimes—almost as often, perhaps, as rewards.

Those are just a few of the beautiful Humming-birds that there are in the world—in that new world that Columbus discovered—but, as you know, there are more than four hundred different kinds, and numbers of them are just as beautiful—some perhaps even more beautiful—than those I have told you about. And you may be sure that they know exactly what to do with their beauty, how to raise up their crests and fan out their tails and ruffle out their gorgets and tippets in the way to make them look most magnificent, and give the greatest possible pleasure to their wives, who are all of them hermits—poor plain Humming-birds—just as the Birds of Paradise do for *their* wives, who are hermits too.

And do you know that when two gentlemen Humming-birds are both trying to please the same lady—but that, of course, is before she has married either of them—they very often fight, and it is then that they gleam and flash and sparkle, more brilliantly than at any other time. Ah, what a wonderful sight that must be to see—those fights between little fiery, winged meteors, those jewel-combats in the air—diamond and ruby and sapphire and topaz and emerald and amethyst, all angry with each other, shooting out sparks at each other, trying to blind each other, to flash each other down! Ah, those are fiery battles indeed, and yet when they are over—you will think it wonderful—not one Humming-bird has been burnt up by another one. No, Humming-birds do not kill each other, they do not even hurt each other very much, they are only angry, and even that does not last very long. *We* are not very angry with the poor Humming-birds, I even think we must be fond of them, for there is really hardly one that we have not called by some pretty name, though not nearly so pretty as itself. And yet we kill them, we take away those bright little gem-like lives that are so lovely and so happy. The people who live in those countries make very fine nets—as fine and delicate as those that ladies use for their hair—and put them over the flowers or the shrubs that the Humming-birds come to, so that they get entangled in them and cannot fly away. Then, when they come and find them, they kill them (could *you* kill a living sunbeam?), and send their skins over here to be put into the hats of women whose hearts the wicked little demon has frozen.

Into hats! Ah, I think if one of those poor, frozen-hearted women could see a Humming-bird, sitting alive in its own little fairy nest, she would blush—yes, *blush*—to think of it in her hat, even though she wore a pretty one and was pretty, herself, too. For I must tell you that the nests that Humming-birds make are so pretty and graceful and delicate that one might almost think they had been made by the fairies, and, indeed, the Indians say that the fairies do make them, and give them to the Humming-birds. But that is not really true. Humming-birds make their own nests, like other birds, though I cannot help thinking that, sometimes, the fairies must sit in them. Yes, they sit and swing in them sometimes, I feel sure, in the warm, tropical nights, when the stars are set thick in the sky and the fire-flies make stars in the air. For they hang like little cradles from the tips of the leaves of palm-trees, or from the ends of long, dangling creepers or tendrils, or even from the drooping petal of a flower. They are made of the fine webs of spiders, all plaited and woven, or of down that is like our thistle-down, but thicker and softer and silkier. And you may think of everything that is soft and delicate and graceful and fragile and fairy-like, but when you see a Humming-bird's nest, you will think them all coarse—yes, *coarse*—by comparison. And to think of that bright little glittering thing, sitting there alive and warm, in its warm little soft fairy nest, and then to think of it in a *hat*—and *dead*! Oh, dear!—dusty too, I feel sure. *Oh*, dear! But it is all the fault of that most wicked little demon, and *you* are going to set it right.

Now perhaps you will wonder why there has been nothing about promising yet, for there have been thirteen Humming-birds in the two last chapters, and not a single promise about any of them. But then, what would be the use of promising about thirteen when there are four hundred and more? It would be ever so much better, *I* think, to promise about all the four hundred and more together, and that is what I want you to ask your mother to do. Then all those little glittering, jewelly, fairy-like things will go on living and being happy—will go on glittering and gleaming, flashing through the air, sparkling amongst the flowers, sitting and shining in dear little soft swinging cradles, on the tips of broad, green palm leaves, or the petals of fair, drooping flowers. They will go on being *living* sunbeams then, not poor, dead, dusty ones in hats. And it will be you who will have done this, you who will have kept sunbeams alive in the world, instead of letting them be killed and go out of it for ever. Yes, it will be you—and your dear mother. So now you must say to your dear mother, "Oh, mother, do promise never to wear a hat that has a Humming-bird in it." Say it quickly, and with *ever* so many kisses.

# CHAPTER X

## THE COCK-OF-THE-ROCK AND THE LYRE-BIRD

Well, I have told you about the Humming-birds and the Birds of Paradise, which are the *most* beautiful birds that there are in the world. Now I will tell you about just a few other ones which are very beautiful, although they are not quite so beautiful as those are. One of them is the Cock-of-the-Rock, a bird which lives in South America, where the Humming-birds live. There are three kinds and they are all handsome, but the handsomest, *I* think, is the one that is called the Blood-red Cock-of-the-Rock. It is about the size of a small pigeon, and of the most wonderful blood-red colour you can imagine. You would think, when you saw it first, that it had not one feather on the whole of its body that was not of this brilliant crimson, but, after a little, when your eyes are not so dazzled, you see that its wings and tail are not red but brown. Only, when the wings are shut they are almost quite covered up by the flaming feathers of the back, and just on one part—that part which we should call the shoulders—they are red too. "A scarlet bird! A crimson bird!" that is what you would say first, if you were to see this wonderful Cock-of-the-Rock, and then, all at once, you would cry out, "Oh, but where is his beak? Why, he has no beak!" Yes, and you might almost say, "Where is his head?" for you don't see that either—at least, you only see the back of it, all the rest, and the beak too, is hidden in a wonderful crest of crimson feathers that almost looks like the head itself, only it is a little too big for that. This crest is just the shape of a tea-cosy, so that it looks as if some one had put a little tea-cosy made of the most splendid blood-red, fiery, crimson-sunset feathers right over the bird's head and covered it quite up. You see no beak at all, and it *does* look so funny to see a bird without a beak—*almost* as funny as it would to see a beak without a bird.

The two other kinds of Cock-of-the-Rock are very handsome birds, too. One of them has all its plumage orange-coloured, instead of crimson, and the other is of a colour between orange and crimson. So, if you were travelling from one part of South America to another, it would seem as if the same bird was getting brighter and brighter or darker and darker all the way, for the three different kinds do not live in the same parts of the country, but in different parts that join each other. Only, of course, you would have to go in the right direction, which would be, first, through the forests of British Guiana, then along the banks of the great river Amazon—which is the largest river in the world—then up the mountains of Peru, and then, still higher, up those of Ecuador. Or, you might start from Ecuador and go all the way to British Guiana. If you get an atlas and look for the map of South America, your mother will soon show you where all these places are.

Now after what you know about the Humming-birds and the Birds of Paradise, you will not be surprised to hear that this brilliant crimson or orange-coloured bird has quite a sober-coloured wife, and that he is as careful to please her, as they are, by showing her his beautiful bright plumage in all the ways in which it looks best; in fact he is so very careful about it that I feel quite sure he pleases himself by doing so, at the same time. You know now that male birds dance, when they show their fine feathers to their wives and sweethearts, for I have told you about the "sácalelis" of the Great Bird of Paradise, and the way in which those other Birds of Paradise danced whilst the two travellers were watching them. But some birds have still more wonderful dances than these; at least they behave in a way that is even more like real dancing. Now the Cock-of-the-Rock is a very fine dancer indeed, and he has a regular place to dance and play in, which we may call his ball-room, or his drawing-room, or his play-ground—whichever name we like best. He chooses it in some part of the forest where it is a little open, and where the ground is soft and mossy, and here, every day, a number of birds assemble, some males and some females; for of course the hen-birds come too, there would be nothing to dance for without them. Then first one of the cocks walks out into the middle of the open space and begins to dance. He flutters and waves his wings, moves his head, with its wonderful crimson tea-cosy, from side to side, and hops about with the queerest little jumpy steps you ever saw. As he goes on he gets more and more excited, springs higher and higher into the air, waves his wings more and more violently, and shakes his head as if he were trying to shake off the tea-cosy, so as to have a cup of tea to refresh himself. All the other birds stand and look at him, criticise his performance, turn their heads towards each other, and make remarks, you may be sure. "How elegant!" exclaims a young hen Cock-of-the-Rock. "What spring! What elasticity! Really he is a very fine performer." "I have seen finer ones in my time," says an older hen—in fact quite an elderly bird. "One could judge better, however, if there were some one else to compare him with. He seems to be having it all his own way. In *my* time there was more emulation amongst male birds." And you may be sure that, as soon as she says that, ever so many other Cocks-of-the-Rock step out into the ring, and there they are, all dancing together, all springing and jumping, all waving their wings, and all trying to shake the tea-cosies off their heads, so as to have a cup of tea for refreshment after all that exercise. Perhaps you will say that that is nonsense, because there is no teapot under the tea-cosy; but remember that no one has ever taken that tea-cosy off. How can you tell what is under a tea-cosy until you take it off. (Your mother will tell you that this is only *fun*.)

But what a strange, curious dance it is, this wonderful bird dance, all in the wild, lonely forest. Oh, how interesting it would be to see it—to find out one of those little, open places where the moss is all pressed smooth and firm, and then to hide somewhere near, and wait there quietly, quietly, without making a sound, all alone in the great, wild, lonely forest, until at last—at last—there is a crimson flash amongst the tree-trunks, and then another and another and another, as bird after bird comes flying or walking to the ball-room, and the dance begins. And sometimes you would see them chasing each other through the forest, all very excited, and often clinging to the trunks of the trees, and spreading and ruffling out their lovely plumage, so as to show it to each other, each one seeming to say, "I *think* mine is finer than yours; *perhaps* I may be mistaken, but I *think* so." What beautiful birds! and what funny birds, and what interesting things they do whilst they are alive! As soon as they are dead they are not funny or interesting any more, and they are only beautiful as a shawl or a piece of embroidery is beautiful. It is dead beauty then; the beauty of life—which is the highest beauty of all—is gone out of them.

**COCK-OF-THE-ROCK**

Now you can see many and many beautiful things that never had life in them, though some, such as beautiful statues and pictures, imitate life so marvellously that you would almost think they were alive. And you can admire these beautiful things, and take pleasure in looking at them, without having to feel sorry that they once were alive and happy, but have been killed for you to look at. Surely you would not wish a beautiful, happy bird to be killed, just for you to look at. You would not even wish it to be put in a cage and kept alive, in a way in which it could not be happy. No, you would rather know that it was alive and happy in its own country, and only imagine what it was like, and how beautiful it was. That is much the best way of seeing creatures, if we have no other way without killing them or putting them in prison—to imagine them; and there is ever so much more pleasure in imagining creatures alive and happy than in seeing them dead or wretched. It is a very fine thing, I can tell you, to *imagine*, and some people can do it a great deal better than others. There *are* people who cannot do it at all, but we do not want birds killed for *stupid* persons. People who cannot imagine can do capitally without seeing, either—just as well as people who *can* imagine, only in another way. Now, just ask your mother to promise not to wear any hat that has the feathers of a beautiful Cock-of-the-Rock in it.

In Australia—oh, but perhaps you want to know why this handsome bird is called the Cock-of-the-Rock, such a very funny name. Well, although it lives in forests and flies about amongst the trees, yet some of these forests are on the sides of mountains, so, of course, there are rocks all about. The Cock-of-the-Rock likes to perch upon a very high one; so, when the old travellers first saw it perched up there, and looking such a fine bird, they called it a Cock-of-the-Rock, and almost expected to hear it crow. At least, if this is not the right explanation, it is the only one I can think of. The Indians *may* have another one, but if they have I cannot tell it you, because I do not know what it is. Perhaps if I were to think a little, I should know—or else I could imagine it—but I have no time to think or imagine just at present. I want to get on.

In Australia, the great island-continent—the island that is so large that we call it a continent—there is a wonderful bird called the Lyre-bird. It is one of the most wonderful and the most beautiful birds that there is in the world, and all its wonder and all its beauty lies in its tail. This wonderful tail—as I am sure you will guess from the name of the bird—is shaped like a lyre, though it is much more beautiful than any lyre ever was, even the one that Apollo played on. You know, I dare say, what a lyre is, a kind of harp with a very graceful shape, curving first out and then in, and then out again on each side, and with the strings in the centre. Now the Lyre-bird has, on each side of its tail, two beautiful, broad feathers that curve in this way, and are of a pretty chestnut colour, with transparent spaces all the way down. These are the two outer tail feathers, and they are like the two sides of the lyre—the solid part of it which is held in the hand, and which we call the framework. Then, for the strings, which, as you know, are stretched across the hollow space within the framework, not from side to side, but lengthways from one end to the other, the Lyre-bird has a number of most beautiful, thin, graceful feathers, more graceful and delicate than the strings of any harp. Only, instead of being straight, like harp strings, these feathers are curved, and droop over to each side in a most graceful way, and instead of keeping inside the two broad feathers—the sides of the lyre—they come a long way past them, and instead of being only four, which is the number of strings that a lyre has, there are ever so many of them—more than a dozen, I feel sure. And if you could see these feathers, and the way they are made, oh, you would think them wonderful. You know that on each side of the quill of most feathers there is what is called the web—which we have talked about—and this web is made of a number of little, light, delicate sprays, like miniature feathers, which we call barbs, and these are kept close together by having a lot of little, tiddy-tiny hooks (though such soft little things don't look like hooks a bit), which are called barbules, with which they catch hold of each other, and won't let each other go. That is why the web of a feather—on each side of the quill—is so smooth and even. But, now, in these wonderful feathers of the Lyre-bird, the little delicate things (the barbs) which make the webs are much fewer than in ordinary feathers, and they have no little hooks to catch hold of each other with, and instead of being all together, they are a quarter of an inch apart, and wave about, each by itself, looking like very delicate threads floating from the long slender quill of the feather. And that, too, is how those beautiful plume-feathers of the Birds of Paradise are formed, and you have seen something like it in the long ones of the peacock's tail. The tail of the Lyre-bird is not so grand, perhaps, as that of the peacock, but it is more graceful and delicate, and on the whole, I *think* (for on such points one can never be sure) it is still more wonderful.

But now is it not very strange that any bird should have a tail like that—a tail that is shaped like Apollo's lyre? Well, I will tell you how it happened, for it is one of those things that requires an explanation—and is lucky. Once the great god Apollo (who is the god of music and song) was walking in Australia and playing upon his lyre. Now, I must tell you, at that time—it was a very long time ago—the Lyre-bird had not a tail like it has now, but quite an ordinary one; so, as it is only its tail that is *extra*ordinary, it was quite an ordinary bird. But although it was ordinary in appearance, it was extremely musical, as it is now—I must tell you that—and also a wonderful imitator of every sound that can be made. The Lyre-bird can imitate all the different notes of other birds, as well as the barking of dogs, the mewing of cats, and the conversation of people.

So, when it heard Apollo playing so sweetly on his lyre, it was quite enraptured, and began to imitate it so cleverly that you would have thought there were two Apollos playing on two lyres. All the other birds and creatures were delighted at this—for, of course, two good things are better than only one—but, for some reason or other which I cannot quite explain, Apollo was not nearly so pleased. In fact, he became angry, and *so* angry that he threw his lyre at the poor bird who had so appreciated his music, and the lyre hit it on the tail as it ran away and cut it right off. Of course, when the Lyre-bird found that it had no tail it was in a terrible state, and it came to Apollo and said: "It was because I loved your music that I tried to imitate it. I failed, no doubt—for who can sing as Apollo?—but still it is a hard price to have to pay for my admiration." And when Apollo heard that, he was so sorry for what he had done, and so pleased with the way in which the Lyre-bird had explained things, that he said to it: "Well, I will make amends, and what I give shall be better than what I took away. The lyre which I threw at you, you shall keep, but it shall be of feathers, and even more beautiful than my own. You shall not play on it, for none but myself must do that, but you shall always be a most musical bird, as you are now, and able to imitate any sound that you hear, even my own playing. That power I will not take away from you, I will even increase it, and from this time forth you shall be called the Lyre-bird, in honour of your piety and good taste."

That is how the Lyre-bird got its tail, and why it is, now, a very beautiful, as well as a very musical, bird. But what its tail was like before Apollo gave it the one it has now, that I cannot tell you, for it has never been known to allude to the subject, and it would hardly do to ask it. We only know that it was quite ordinary. But, do you know, Apollo never quite liked the Lyre-bird's imitating him, even though he had told it that it might, and so, not so very long afterwards, he left the country. He went to Greece—it was a very long time ago—and he has not gone back to Australia yet.

Now you may be sure that a bird with a tail like that has his playing ground, where he may come and show it to his wife or sweetheart; for it is only the male bird who has it—like the others—though, really, I cannot think what Apollo was about, not to give it to the hen as well, for he was always a very polite god. The Lyre-bird's playground is a small, round hillock—which he makes all himself—and there he will come and walk about, raising his magnificent tail right up into the air, and spreading it out in the most beautiful and graceful way. And, as he does this, he will sing so beautifully, sometimes his own notes, which are very pretty ones, and sometimes those of other birds, all of which he can imitate quite well. But, of course, as Apollo has left Australia, he cannot imitate him any more now, and after such a long time he has forgotten what he learnt, unless, indeed, his own notes are what Apollo used to play. But, if that is the case, he must have left off singing his old song, and I do not think he would have done that.

This wonderful bird builds a wonderful nest with a roof to it, so that he can get right inside it and be quite hidden from sight, tail and all, although he is so large—almost as large as a pheasant, even without counting his tail. As a rule it is only little birds that make nests like that, and not big ones. The Lyre-bird's nest is something like the one that our little wren makes—which perhaps you have seen—only of course ever so much bigger. Only one egg is laid in it, and out of it comes one of the queerest little birds you can imagine, all covered with white, fluffy down, and with no tail at all that you can see, so that you would never think he was going to grow into a Lyre-bird. It takes him four years to get that wonderful tail. Apollo did not mean him to have it, until he was quite grown up—it was not a thing to be entrusted to children.

Now you must not think that the Lyre-bird always holds his tail up in the air, for when he walks through the thick bushes he has to carry it as a pheasant does, and I think you know how that is. As soon as he wants to show it to his wife or his sweetheart, up it goes, and oh, it *does* look so beautiful!

But now, if it were not for that promise which your mother is going to make you, there would very soon be no more of these wonderful birds, with their wonderful and beautiful tails, left in Australia, which would mean that there would be none in the whole world, for Australia is the only country in the world where they are found. People like much better to see that beautiful tail in their rooms, where it will soon get spoilt and dusty, or to put some feathers of it in their hats, than to know that the bird is running about with it, alive and happy, holding it down like a pheasant's when he walks through the bushes, but raising it in the air when he stands on his little hillock, for the hen Lyre-bird to see, and singing her a song as well. People who live in Australia—and there are a great many people who live there—might often see it doing that if they were to take a little trouble (they take a great deal of trouble to kill it), and, even if they could not see it, they would hear its beautiful song. But they like much better to kill it, so that there may be a little less song and beauty and happiness in the world, and all because of the wicked little demon with the correct suit of clothes. But all this is going to be altered, and you are going to alter it. Just run to your mother, wherever she is—if she is not with you now—and ask her to promise, *ever* so faithfully, never to have anything whatever to do with a hat that has so much as one single feather of a Lyre-bird in it.

# CHAPTER XI

## THE RESPLENDENT TROGON AND THE ARGUS PHEASANT

One of the most beautiful birds in the whole world—more beautiful, even, than *some* of the Birds of Paradise and than *some* of the Humming-birds, even those that are not hermits—is the lovely Trogon of Mexico. But first I must tell you that there are a great many birds called Trogons that live in other parts of America as well as in Mexico, and in other parts of the world as well as in America. But the most beautiful of all of them—which is the only one I shall have time to tell you about—is the Resplendent Trogon or Quezal—for that is what the Indians call it— and it is only found in Mexico, which, you know, is in North America, only right down at the southern end of it, where there are a good many Humming-birds too. There are many more Humming-birds in South America than in North America. It is the hot, tropical countries they are so fond of. You see they like to be with their brothers the sunbeams.

This Mexico is such an interesting country. It belongs, now, to the Spaniards, whom I dare say you have heard about, but once it belonged to a quite different people, an old people who had been there for hundreds and hundreds of years, long before Columbus discovered America. These people were civilised, only in a different way to ourselves. They did not wear the kind of clothes that we do, but only light linen things, dyed all sorts of colours, which were prettier and suited the climate. They had many cities, as we have, though they were built in a different way, and the largest was built all over a great lake, with bridges going from one side of it to another. One can build houses in the water, you know, for there is Venice in Italy, and Rotterdam in Holland, which are both built in the sea, and which your mother will tell you about.

These people, who were called Aztecs, were very clever workmen, and such wonderful goldsmiths and silversmiths, especially, that they used to make imitation gardens, with all sorts of flowers beaten out of gold and silver. Then they used feathers as we do a paint-box, to make pictures of things with. They would paint houses and ships and men and boats and landscapes with them, putting the right-coloured feathers just where they were wanted, blue ones for the sky, green ones for the grass, and so on. For the wicked little demon knew of those people just as well as he knows of us, and he had taught them to kill birds, too. Only as they had no guns they could not kill nearly so many of them as we can, so that there was no danger, then, of a beautiful bird getting rarer and rarer, until, at last, it is not to be found in the world any more, which is what happens now with us—at least it will if *you* do not stop it. But though it would have been much better to let these birds—which were often Humming-birds—go on living and flying about, and though no picture made with their feathers was nearly so beautiful as the feathers themselves were, growing upon them, yet these feather-pictures of the old Aztecs were very wonderful things, and it is a great pity that there are none of them left now, for us to look at. Nothing could bring the poor birds back to life, so we might just as well have had the pictures that they had helped to make.

And we might have had some other pictures, too, that these people made, for they used to draw things, just as we do, and when they wanted to describe a thing they would often draw a picture of it, instead of only *saying* what it was like. Even their writing was all in pictures, for when they wanted to write—say the word "sun" or the word "house"—they would draw a little picture of the sun or of a house, only so quickly and with such a few strokes of the pen or the paint-brush (I don't quite know which it was), that it was quite like proper writing. Of course there are some words that are not so easy to make a picture of—as you can try for yourself—but, wherever it could be done, these old Aztecs would do it. And if only we had some more of this writing (for we have very little of it), we should be able to know a great deal more about this old people, who were in America before Columbus came there, and what they did and what they thought about, and the remarks they made to each other, and just think how interesting that would be. It is always interesting to know something about people quite different to ourselves who lived a long time ago.

Unfortunately, when the Spaniards had conquered these people, instead of keeping the things which they had made, they burnt them. They burnt their houses, their temples, their cities, their picture-writings, their feather-pictures, their wonderful flowers—until the gold and silver they were made of were quite melted—their clothes, everything—even the people themselves—and, to save time, they often burnt the two last together. It is a great pity they did this, but, you see, everybody has a plan of doing things, and the plan of the Spaniards was to burn the people they conquered, and everything belonging to them. But was it not horribly cruel? Oh! most horribly; but so it is to shoot sea-gulls, and then to cut off their wings, before they are dead, and throw them back into the sea, to drown there or bleed to death. That is what *we* do, and *it* is horribly cruel, too. So do not let us think about the cruel things the Spaniards did—yet. Let us think, first, about the cruel things that are done by people in our own country, and try to stop *them*. *When* we have stopped them—*all* of them—then we can think about the Spaniards—and some other nations.

You know there is a proverb which says, "Those who live in glass houses should not throw stones;" that is generally one of the first proverbs we learn, and *always* the very first one we forget. I am afraid that those old Aztecs lived in *rather* a glass house, for *they* had a plan of cutting people open, whilst they were still alive, and tearing their hearts out. Horrible! was it not? But they did not *burn* people; so, when they saw the Spaniards doing so, they were shocked at them. As for the Spaniards, *they* were shocked at the Aztecs doing this other thing, for *that* had never been *their* custom. So the Aztecs and the Spaniards were shocked at each other. People are very easily shocked at each other, but they are not nearly so easily shocked at themselves. Now I come to think of it, I never remember hearing any one say, "I am *shocked* at myself!" And yet it would often be a quite sensible remark.

But what I wanted to tell you about these old Aztecs, who lived in Mexico all that time ago, was that, when the Spaniards came there, they were ruled over by a great king named Montezuma, and this king, amongst many other wonderful things, had a great place, where he kept all the different kinds of birds that were found in his country. A place like that is called an aviary, and you may be quite sure that the beautiful Trogon or Quezal was one of the birds in King Montezuma's aviary, for it was more highly thought of than any other bird in the country. Let us hope that all the birds in this aviary had nice, large places to be in, with trees, and flowers, and everything that they wanted; and, as it was a king's aviary, I daresay they had.

Well, now, I will tell you what this beautiful bird, the Quezal or Resplendent Trogon, that used to be in King Montezuma's aviary, is like. It is about the size of a turtle-dove, but with the most beautiful, long, curling feathers in its tail, and these beautiful feathers, and all the feathers on its back and breast and on its head, too, are of the most lovely, rich, golden-green colour. Really I don't know whether there is more of gold or of green in them, but there is just the right quantity of each to make them the most beautiful, beautiful feathers you can possibly imagine. It is the tail-feathers that are the most beautiful, for they are so very long—the two longest are much longer than those in a pheasant's tail—but there are some feathers which begin on the back and lap softly round the sides, one a little way off from the other, so that you see their pretty shapes, and these are almost as beautiful, although they are ever so much shorter. But now there is something funny about those long feathers, which I have called the tail-feathers, and that is, that they are not *really* tail-feathers at all. They look as if they were, but *really* they are feathers which go *over* the tail and cover it up, so that the *real* tail is underneath them. It is like that—though I am sure you never knew it—with the peacock; those beautiful, long feathers which we *call* the tail are not *really* the tail, and you will see that, directly, if you watch a peacock when he spreads them out, for, as soon as he does, you will see the real tail underneath, which is nothing very particular to look at. Still, in both these birds the long feathers look so like the real tail that we may very well call them the tail-feathers, and we can always explain about it afterwards, to show how much we know. And, do you know, these beautiful, long, golden-green feathers of the Quezal, which we are going to call the tail-feathers, although we know very well they are not, were so highly valued by these people who used to live in Mexico, that no one was ever allowed to kill the bird, but only to catch it and cut them off and let it go again, so that new ones might grow on it. And only the chiefs were allowed to wear its feathers. And, indeed, there would be no great harm in wearing feathers in hats, if we got them only in that way. Only I cannot think what the little demon could have been about in that country. A law like that must have made him very angry indeed.

Then, besides his splendid tail-feathers, this beautiful bird has a crest on his head, which is something like the one the Cock-of-the-Rock has on his, for it is of the same tea-cosy shape, only it is green instead of crimson, and it does not quite cover up the beak. So perhaps you will think that, as the Cock-of-the-Rock is all blood-red, with a tea-cosy crest on his head, this beautiful golden-green Trogon, with the tea-cosy crest on *his* head, is all golden-green. But no, all the lower part of him—that part which is hidden when he sits down—instead of being golden-green, is the most splendid vermilion, as bright a colour—although it is not quite the same—as the Cock-of-the-Rock's himself. Just think, golden-green and splendidly bright vermilion! and you cannot think how beautiful the one looks against the other. Whether they would look quite so well together in a dress *I* am not quite sure, but your mother would know all about that. Only you must remember that *such* a golden-green and *such* a vermilion as this Trogon has were never seen together—no, or separately either—in any dress yet.

**THE RESPLENDENT TROGON**

These beautiful Quezals live in the forests of Mexico, and they like to sit lazily on the branch of a tree, and let their beautiful long tails (which we know are not *really* tails) hang down underneath it, like the "funny feathers" of the Birds of Paradise. At least the male birds like to do that, because the female Quezals have not got those beautiful, long feathers, although they are very fine birds even without them. They are not so handsome as the males, but they are not plain like the female Humming-birds or Birds of Paradise. Perhaps the male Quezals show off their fine feathers to the females by letting them hang down like that, because, of course, long, soft, drooping feathers, such as they have, would not stand up in the air, like those of the peacock or of the Lyre-bird. But very likely they have some other nice way of showing them.

Now, although the Quezal or Resplendent Trogon is such a magnificent bird, he is not so very often seen. It is difficult to find him in the dense forest, and I wish it was still more difficult than it is, for when he *is* found, he is always shot for those beautiful feathers of his. When the Indian who is looking for him sees him sitting in the way I have told you, he hides somewhere near and imitates the cry of the bird. When the poor Trogon hears it, he thinks it is another Trogon—a friend of his, perhaps—and so he comes flying to where the sound came from. Then this deceitful man—and I really think it is *very* contemptible to deceive a bird in that way—shoots him, and there is one beautiful, happy bird less in the world. Is it not dreadful to think of, that in almost every part of the world there are some *very* beautiful birds to be found, and everywhere they are being killed and killed and killed, so that they are getting scarcer and scarcer every year? If it were not for what your mother has promised you about the Lyre-bird, and what she is going to promise you about this Trogon, there would soon be no more beautiful Lyre-birds in Australia, and no more beautiful Trogons in Mexico. How terrible that would be! But we have saved the beautiful Lyre-bird, and now we are going to save the beautiful Trogon. Ask your mother—oh, *do* ask her—to promise, most *faithfully*, never to have anything whatever to do with a hat that has any of the feathers—short or long, golden-green or vermilion—of a Quezal—a Resplendent Trogon—in it. Ah, now she has promised, and we have saved that beautiful bird as well as a great many others.

Now I will tell you about a very beautiful pheasant—the Argus Pheasant. Some people may think him the most beautiful one of all. And yet he is not the most showy pheasant—for the pheasants, you know, are very showy birds indeed. There is the Golden Pheasant, who is dressed in the sun's own livery; and the Silver Pheasant, who has a silver white one which is more like the moon's, but who looks gaudy and smart all the same; and the Amherst Pheasant, who manages to be handsomer than both the sun and moon—which is very clever of him; and the Fire-back, who is all in a blaze without minding it at all; and the Impeyan or Monal, who looks as if he was made of beaten metal, and had just been polished up with a piece of wash-leather. There is the Peacock, too—for he is really nothing but a large pheasant—so, you see, the pheasants are a handsome family, and you may be sure that they know how to appreciate themselves. The pheasant that we are going to talk about is quite a large bird, not so large as the peacock, it is true, but with still longer tail-feathers, and oh, such wonderful wings! One may say, indeed, that this bird is all wings and tail, but he is principally wings, at least when he spreads them out. But, even when they are folded, they are so very large that he looks quite wrapped up in them; and I think he is, too, partly because of that, but still more because they are so very handsome.

So, first, I will tell you what these large, handsome wings of his are like. Well, in each one there are twenty-five or twenty-six very fine long feathers, but these feathers are not all so fine or so long as each other. Ten of them are about a foot long, and these are prettily marked and mottled with all sorts of pretty brown colours, whilst, down the centre of each one, there is a pretty blue stripe. It is the quill of the feather that makes that stripe, for it is blue, and looks as if it had been painted. So you see even these are pretty feathers, but it is the fifteen or sixteen other ones that are so very beautiful. They are much broader and longer than the other ten—the longest are more than twice as long—and down each of them, just on one side of the great quill in the centre, there is a row of such wonderful spots. They are as large as horse-chestnuts (big ones I mean), and what they look like is a cup and ball, the ball just lying in the cup ready to be sent up; only, of course, the cup has no handle to it—you must not think that—for the spots are round. And, do you know, the balls look as if they were *really* balls, so that you would think you could take them in your hand, and throw them up into the air, and catch them again as they came down. They do not look flat at all. You know, when you try to draw an orange or an apple, how difficult it is not to make it look flat like a penny. *You would* make it look flat, I know, but these wonderful balls on the Argus Pheasant's feathers look as if they had all been drawn by a very clever artist (as indeed they have been—a *very* clever one), who had shaded them properly; you know how difficult shading is. There are eighteen or twenty—sometimes as many as twenty-two—of these wonderful spots on each feather, but I have not told you, yet, of what colour they are. Perhaps you will think they are very bright and dazzling. No, they are not like that at all. They are soft, not bright, and their softness is their beauty. All round them, at the edge, there is a ring of deep, soft brown, and, just inside the ring, there is a lighter brown, and it goes on getting lighter and lighter, until, in the centre, it is a pretty, soft amber, and, at the edge of the soft amber, there is a pretty, white, silvery light, as if the moon was just coming out from behind an amber cloud. *So* pretty! And when the Argus Pheasant spreads his wonderful wings out, you can see more than a hundred of these wonderful spots on each wing, which is more than two hundred altogether. Such a sight! so soft and so pretty they look. Shall I tell you what such wings are like? They are like skies where the stars are all moons, that float softly among soft brown and amber clouds, tipping them all with soft silver. For the Argus Pheasant is not one of the very brilliant birds of the world. No, he is not brilliant at all. His colours are only soft browns and soft ambers and soft, silver whites, and yet he is so pretty, so beautiful. I think he is as pretty as the peacock, and, when one sees him after the peacock, it is a rest for the eye. Some people might prefer him to the peacock. Do you wonder at that? It is not so very wonderful. There may be a little girl reading this, with soft brown hair and soft brown eyes, and with nothing golden or gleaming about her, and some people, besides her father and mother, may think her prettier than the little girl who is all golden and gleaming. It is all a matter of taste. Some like a broad sheet of water dancing in the sunlight, and some like quiet streams running under cool, mossy banks, with trees arching above them, where the shadows are cool and deep, and where even the sun's peepings are only like brighter shadows. People who like that better than the other, will like the quiet little girl with the brown hair better than the one who gleams and dazzles; and they will like the Argus Pheasant better than the peacock, and think them both a rest for the eye. It is not at all a bad thing to be a rest for the eye.

## THE ARGUS PHEASANT

I have told you how large the wings of the Argus Pheasant are; when he spreads them out to show to the hen bird (who has nothing like them), they look like two banners or two beautiful feather-fans, the kind of fans that you see Eastern queens being fanned with, in the pictures. Then he has a very fine tail as well, as I told you. Two of the feathers in it are very long indeed—quite four feet long, I should think—and as broad as a man's hand, if not broader, near the base (which means where they begin), but getting gradually narrower towards the tips. On one side, these feathers are a soft, rich brown, with silver-white spots, and, on the other, a soft, silver grey, with silver-white spots. When the Argus Pheasant spreads out his two great wings, he takes care to lift up his fine handsome tail, as well, so that the two long feathers of it are quite high in the air. So there is his tail going up like a rocket, whilst his wings spread out on each side of it, like feather-fans, and his head comes out between them, just in the middle, and makes a polite bow to the hen. That is the right way to do it, and the Argus Pheasant would rather not do it at all than not do it properly. Oh, he takes a great deal of trouble about it, and all for the hen—which is unselfish.

This beautiful Argus Pheasant lives in Sumatra—which is a large island of the Malay Archipelago—and also in the Malay Peninsula and Siam, which are, both, part of the great Asiatic continent—as perhaps you know. Yes, that is where he lives, but you might walk about there for a very long time, without ever once seeing him, for the Argus Pheasant is a very difficult bird to find. He lives in the great, thick forests, and keeps out of everybody's way. One hardly ever does find *him*, but, sometimes, one finds his drawing-room (for he has one, like the Cock-of-the-Rock and the Lyre-bird), and if one waits there long enough (*I* would wait a week if it were necessary) one may see him come into it. He spends almost all his time in looking after this drawing-room, and he only sees the hen Argus Pheasant when she comes there too, to look at him. Of course he dances in it, and it is there that he spreads out his wonderful wings and lifts up his tail, in the way that I have told you. The Argus Pheasant is very proud of his drawing-room, and he *will* have it nice and clean, with nothing lying about in it. So, if he finds anything there that has no business to be there, he picks it up with his beak, and throws it outside. He has not to open a door to do that; his drawing-room is only an open space which he keeps nice and smooth, so, as it is always open, it does not want a door to it. Now I think you will say—and I am *sure* your mother will agree with you—that the Argus Pheasant does quite right to act in this way, and that to keep one's drawing-room clean and tidy is a very proper thing to do. Your mother may be surprised, perhaps, that it is the male Argus Pheasant, and not the hen bird, that does it, but I am sure she will not blame *him* on that account. But I am sorry to say that the wicked little demon has found out a way of making this habit of the poor bird's—which is such a good one—a means of killing him.

The people who live in that part of the world—those yellow people called Malays that I have told you of—know all about the ways of the Argus Pheasant, and how he will *not* have things lying about in his drawing-room. Now there is a great tall reed that grows there, called the bamboo, which I am sure you have heard of, and which your mother will tell you all about. The Malays cut off a piece of this bamboo, about two feet long, and then they shave it down—all except about six inches at one end of it—till it is almost as thin as writing paper. It looks like a piece of ribbon then, only, as it is very hard, as well as thin, its edges are quite sharp, and able to cut like a razor. But the piece at the end, which has been left and not shaved down, they cut into a point, so that it makes a peg, and this peg, that has a ribbon at the end of it, they stick into the ground, right in the middle of the Argus Pheasant's drawing-room. So, when the poor Argus Pheasant comes into his drawing-room, he sees something lying on the floor, which has no business to be there. It may be only a ribbon, but that is not the right place for it, so he tries to pick it up and throw it outside. But it won't come, however much he pulls it, for the peg at the end is fixed in the ground, and he is not strong enough to pull it out. At last he gets angry and thinks he will make a great effort. He twists the long ribbon round and round his neck—just as you would twist a piece of string round and round your hand if you were going to pull it hard—then takes hold of it with his beak, just above the ground, and gives quite a tremendous spring backwards. You may guess what happens. The long peg does not come out of the ground, but the ribbon is drawn quite tight round the poor bird's own neck, and the sharp edges almost cut his head off.

Now is not *that* a most cruel trick to play upon a bird who only wants to keep his drawing-room in proper order? How would your dear mother like to be treated in such a way for being *neat* and *tidy*, which I am sure she is? But we are going to stop it—this cruel trick of the wicked little demon—for it was he who thought of it and taught it to the Malays. It is not *their* fault, you must not be angry with them, any more than with the poor women whose hearts the same demon has frozen. We are going to stop it, and you know how. The Malay only kills the poor Argus Pheasant to sell his feathers. If *they* were not wanted he would leave him alone, to be happy and beautiful, and to dance in a nice tidy drawing-room. So just ask your mother to promise never to wear a hat—or anything else—that has a feather, or even a little piece of a feather, of an Argus Pheasant in it.

That was going to be the end of the chapter, but there is just something which I have forgotten. I am sure you will have been wondering why this beautiful pheasant is called the Argus Pheasant, and what the word Argus means. Well, I will give you an explanation. Argus was the name of a wonderful being—a kind of monster—who had a hundred eyes, and who lived a long time ago. But he offended the great god Jupiter, who had him killed, and then Jupiter's wife—the goddess Juno—whose servant he was, put all his eyes into the tail of the peacock—for the peacock was her favourite bird. That is one story; but another one says that she did *not* put them *all* there, but only the bright ones. The soft ones—those pretty ones that I have been telling you about—she put into the wings of another bird, that she liked quite as well, if not better, and that bird became, at once, the Argus Pheasant. But now if Argus had only a hundred eyes, how is it that there are two hundred, or more, in the wings of the Argus Pheasant, to say nothing of those in the tail of the peacock? That shows, *I* think, quite clearly that he must, really, have had a great many more; and so, now, when people talk to you of Argus and his hundred eyes, you can say, "A hundred, indeed! Why, he must have had *three* hundred at the very least." And then you can tell them why.

# CHAPTER XII

## WHITE EGRETS, "OSPREYS," AND OS-TRICH-FEATHERS

The last bird I am going to tell you about is the White Egret. But, do you know, I am not quite sure if he is beautiful enough to be put in a book of beautiful birds, because, of course, a book of beautiful birds means a book of *the* most beautiful birds that there are, and I am not *quite* sure if the White Egret is so beautiful as all that. At any rate he is not so beautiful as the birds I have been telling you about, and there are many other birds in the world that I have *not* told you about, that are more beautiful than he is. So, perhaps, you will wonder why I put him into the book at all, but I will soon give you a proper explanation of it. In the first place, if the White Egret is not one of the most beautiful birds in the world, yet, at any rate, he has some of the most beautiful feathers that any bird has, and that alone, I think, gives him a right to be here, because, you know, "fine feathers make fine birds." And, in the second place, this poor bird is so shot and killed and persecuted for these beautiful feathers of his, that, unless you were to get your mother to make that promise about him, there would soon be no such thing as a White Egret left in the world. He and his feathers would both be gone.

But now, perhaps, you will say that if "fine feathers make fine birds," then beautiful feathers must make beautiful birds, too, and so the White Egret must be a beautiful bird. Oh, yes, he is. You are quite right. I did not mean that he was not a beautiful bird at all. All I meant was that he was not quite so beautiful as the Birds of Paradise and the Humming-birds, and birds like that—birds that look as if they had flown into a jeweller's shop, and then flown out again with all the best part of the jewellery upon them. Whether he is not as beautiful as some of the other birds we have talked about—but I will not say which, for fear of offending them—that I am not quite so sure of; but, at any rate, he is beautiful.

Oh, yes, he is quite a beautiful bird, is the White Egret; and now I will describe him to you. I shall not have any colours to tell you about, because he is all white—which of course you will have guessed from his name—but you know how beautiful white can be. You will not have forgotten the little Humming-bird who was made still more beautiful than he had been before, by three snowflakes falling upon him. But, with this bird, it is as if the snow had fallen all over him and covered him up, for he is white all over, a beautiful, soft, silky white, as pure and delicate as the snow itself. Only his shape, perhaps, is a little funny—at least you might think so—for he has a pair of long, thin, stilty legs, and a long, thin, snaky neck, and a long, sharp, pointed beak, so that all three of these together make him a tall, thin, stilty bird. "Something like a stork, that is," you will say, for you will have seen pictures of storks, even if you have not seen one alive in the Zoological Gardens—which is a very bad place for him, *I* think. Well, this bird *is* something like a stork, but he is a great deal more like a heron, that long-legged, long-necked bird that stands for hours in the water, waiting for a fish to come near it, so that it may catch it and swallow it; for the heron, you know, lives on fish and frogs, and things of that sort.

**THE WHITE EGRET**

Yes, he is very like a heron, and, do you know, there is a very good reason for that, because the White Egret *is* a heron. Some birds, I must tell you, have names which are like our surnames, and show the family they belong to. As long as you only know a boy's or girl's Christian name—Reginald or Bertram or Dorothy or Norah or Wilhelmina—you don't know a bit what family they belong to; but as soon as you know their *surnames*—Smith or Brown or Jones or Thompson or Robinson—why then you do—and it is just the same with birds. Heron is really a surname, only the bird that has it, here in England, has not a Christian name as well—unless "common" is one, for he is called the Common Heron. But White Egret is a Christian name and the surname to it is Heron—for the White Egret belongs to the Heron family. That is why he is so tall and gaunt and stilty, for a heron is always like that—it is the family figure—and so now, when I tell you that *he* stands in the water and catches fish, you will know why he does that, too; fish is the family dish, and no heron would think of going without it, for long.

But now, let me tell you about those beautiful feathers which the poor White Egret has. They grow only on his back—about the middle of it—and droop down to a little way over his tail, so that they are a foot or more long. You remember what I explained to you about the feathers in the tail of the Lyre-bird, and those that make the plumes in the beautiful Birds of Paradise—how the barbs of the feather on each side of the quill have no barbules to hold them together, so that they fall apart and wave about like beautiful, soft, silky threads. If you have forgotten, then you must look back for it, because I should not explain it better here than I do there, and, besides, it would be twice over. Well, these feathers are made in the same way, only they are of a pure, shining white—like all the rest of this birds plumage—and although they are as soft as silk they are stiff at the same time, and so smooth that they look like the delicate flakings from a piece of beautiful, pure, polished ivory. Imagine a little fountain of ivory threads all shooting up together into the air, quite straight at first, and then bending over and drooping down in the most delicate, graceful way imaginable. That is what a plume of those feathers looks like, when they have been taken out and tied together, but I wish, myself, that they did not look nearly so beautiful, for it is because of those beautiful plumes, that the poor bird is being killed and killed and becoming scarcer and scarcer, every day. For the women whose hearts the little demon has frozen, wear these plumes in their hats and in their hair, and they are called "ospreys," and are very fashionable indeed.

Soldiers, too, used to wear them in their caps, but *they* have given up doing so. It is only the frozen-hearted women who are killing the poor White Egrets now—but ah, there are so many of them (the women I mean, not the Egrets). I have sat at the entrance of a large concert-hall, and counted the faces that had these lovely egret-plumes—these beautiful, fashionable "ospreys," so white and yet so blood-stained—nodding above them—counted them as they came in and as they went out, young faces, old faces, soft faces, hard faces, shrivelled faces, puckered faces, painted faces, plain faces, ugly faces, quite dreadful faces—ah, what numbers of them there were! It was quite difficult to count them all. Every now and again there would be a pretty face, and I used to count *those* separately—one—two—three—four—five—sometimes up to half-a-dozen. That was not so tiring, but, you see, I had to count them all.

Oh, wise but wicked little demon, who blew his bad powders into the hearts of *all* the women! There were two kinds, you know, and one of them was "Vanity." Now if it had been a man—however wicked a one—I feel sure that he would have looked about for the women with the *pretty* faces, and who were rather young, to blow *that* powder into. But the little demon was wiser, in his own wicked way. He did not go about, looking and looking. He blew it into *all* their hearts, and that gave him no trouble at all.

Now, I must tell you that there are two different kinds of White Egrets, with these beautiful feathers that the women with the frozen hearts wear. One is much larger than the other, and is called the Great White Egret. He is quite a big bird, larger even than our common heron—and you know what a big bird *he* is. The other one, which is called the Small White Egret, is not more than half the size of the great one, but his feathers are the most beautiful, so that, though he has not nearly so many of them, he is worth nearly twice as much money. That means, of course, that the servants of the wicked little demon, who shoot him and sell his feathers, can get nearly twice as much money for them as they can for the feathers of the other one. So, of course, they like shooting him best, but they are very glad to shoot the other one—the Great White Egret—too, for even *his* feathers are worth a good deal. Now, if the wicked little demon had not frozen the hearts of women, they would never want to wear feathers that cost the lives of the poor birds to whom they belong—because, you know, women are, *really*, so kind. Then, of course, those feathers that are so beautiful would not be worth anything (as it is called), and so men would not shoot the White Egrets, because they would not be able to sell their feathers. I am afraid they would have no better reason for not doing so than that, because men, you know, are not kind and pitiful—as women are, if only their hearts are not frozen. But, at any rate, the White Egrets would be left alive.

And you must not think that their feathers would *really* not be worth anything, then. When we talk of a thing not being worth anything, what we really mean is that we cannot sell it for money. Now what are things that you cannot sell for money? I will tell you three. There is the sky, and the air, and the sunlight. You cannot buy or sell them, but do you think they are not worth anything! *I* think they are worth a good deal. Then there is a good temper; nobody can buy that, but yet what a lot it is worth! Now if the beautiful feathers of the White Egret could not be sold, because the world was better and there were no frozen-hearted women to buy them, yet they would be worth something, although it would not be money. They would be worth love and pity and sympathy and interest and real admiration (which never wants to kill), for all those things would be given to the beautiful bird with its beautiful feathers, and it would be just because of those things that no one would think of killing him. His feathers, then, would be like the smiles on a face. You cannot take those *out* of the face, and put them in a hat. If you could, then some one would soon say to you: "Will you part with a few of your smiles? They are fashionable in hats just now; I will give you, for a nice, bright one—let me see—half-a-crown." Then you might say that a nice, bright smile was worth half-a-crown. But I think it is worth much more where it is, in your face, though you cannot take it out and get half-a-crown for it.

Smiles are not bought for money in *that* way, but you must remember that what is not worth money is often worth much better things. That is why I wish the feathers of the poor White Egrets were not worth even a penny. If they were not, then, if you were to go to the countries where they live, you would see those feathers on the birds themselves, where they look most beautiful, and you could watch the birds (with the feathers on them) flying through the air, or perched in trees, or walking about in the water and catching fish in it, or building their nests, or feeding their young, or doing all sorts of other interesting and amusing things. And they would not be so rare then; in fact they would be quite common, so that you would not have to go into such out-of-the-way places—yes, and such unhealthy places too—in order to see them. No, they would be all about, so that they would often come to see *you*, instead of your going to see *them*; sometimes, even, they might come into your garden—for why should you not have a garden in another country?—and walk about on the lawn. Think how interesting that would be, and how pretty it would look!—and all because those beautiful white feathers would not be worth anything.

But, because they are worth a good deal, men who would kill every bird in the world for money go out with guns, and shoot these poor White Egrets whenever and wherever they see them. And, because of this, they are only to be found, now, in swamps and places where you, and most other sensible people, do not like to go; so that, now, the only people who ever see these beautiful birds are just the servants of the demon, who murder them as soon as they see them. You and I, and others like us, who would like to look at them, and admire them, and watch their ways, and learn all about them, cannot do so, cannot see them at all, cannot even imagine them, unless in swamps, and being shot. Yet once they were quite common, so that everybody might look at them. Now they are getting rarer and rarer, so that very soon, if we do not do something about it quickly, there will be no more of them left in the world. How dreadful that is to think of! If you were to see a very beautiful picture, or statue, and then, afterwards, you were to hear that it had been destroyed, you would feel sorry, would you not? And not only you, but all the world would. I feel perfectly sure that if Sir Edwin Landseer, who (as your mother will tell you) was a great animal artist, had painted a White Egret, everybody would think it quite shocking if it were to be burnt or torn up. You would hear people say (and they would be quite right to say so): "Oh, it is dreadful, it is quite dreadful to think of! It can never be replaced! There is no such other artist! To think of such a masterpiece being destroyed!" Now, when all the White Egrets (and let me tell you they are *all* masterpieces) have been destroyed, it will be quite impossible to replace any one of them; so that that kind of bird—or any other kind of bird or animal that has been shot and shot till there are no more of it left—will have gone in just the same way that a picture goes, when you burn it or tear it to pieces. But is there any picture of a bird or animal, that is so beautiful or so wonderful as that bird or animal itself? And is there any artist so great as the artist who made it, who made that bird or animal, that picture with a life inside it? You know who *that* artist is, you know *His* name—or if you do not, your mother will tell you. I have called Him Dame Nature, but that is only just a way of talking. He has another name, greater than that. He is a much greater artist than Sir Edwin Landseer (or even Raphael or Phidias), but I am afraid there are not many people who really know that He is. Perhaps He is too great to be appreciated. That sometimes happens, even amongst ourselves.

Well, these poor White Egrets—these masterpieces that are always being destroyed—are birds that live, mostly, in America—in Mexico, and California, and Florida, and, I think, all over South and Central America. They live in the swamps and lagunes—as they are called—of the great forests, where trees grow all about in the water—such dark, gloomy, wonderful places—and the servants of the little demon, whose business it is to kill them, have to follow them to those places, and live there, too. Of course it is very unhealthy for them, and they often die there; but the women with the frozen hearts do not mind that, any more than they mind the Egrets being shot. They want the feathers, and when they pay for the feathers they pay for the lives as well—for they are honest, although their hearts have been frozen.

Perhaps you will wonder how men can live at all, in such places as those. Of course, as it is all water, they have to live in boats or canoes, and as soon as they have found out a pool or creek, where the White Egrets come to catch fish, or some trees where they have built their nests, they cover their boats over with reeds or rushes or ferns or the branches of trees, so that, even though you were to come quite close to them, you would not think they were boats at all, but only part of the forest. That is what the poor White Egrets think, for the men sit in their covered-up boats, quite silently—without speaking a word—and, as soon as they come near enough to them, fire at them and kill them.

And now I will tell you another dreadful thing, which makes the killing of these poor birds more cruel even than you will have thought it was, though I am sure you will have thought it cruel enough. I have spoken of their having nests, so, of course, there will often be young ones in those nests, who cannot feed themselves, but have to be fed by the parent birds. What do the young ones do when the parent birds—their own fathers and mothers—have been shot? I will tell you. They starve. That is what they do, and that is what the women with the frozen hearts, who wear these feathers, know that they do—for they have been told so, now, often enough. Is it not terrible? For those pure, white, beautiful feathers, not only have the grown birds been killed, but the young ones—their children— have starved—starved slowly—in the nest where they were born. Day after day they had looked out from it, to see their father or mother come flying to them, with something to eat; day after day they had not seen them, and when the night came—oh, they were so hungry! Before, how glad they used to be when they saw the great, white wings come floating to them, slowly, through the air, like a silver sun, like a broad, white, silken sail. Nearer and nearer they came, and then there was a cry of greeting, and such *good* appetites for breakfast or dinner. Their appetites were just as good now—indeed better, for they were starving—but where was father or mother, where were the broad, white wings, the silken sail, the great silver sun? Oh, how they strained their eyes and stretched their poor, little, long necks over the side of the nest, to try to see them, to see if they were not coming, if there was only a speck of white in the distance! But they saw nothing, for father and mother had both been shot. And, now, they grew so weak with hunger that they could not hold their heads up, any more. They laid them down in the nest, and their eyes closed, and their poor little voices only came in whispers, "Feed us! feed us!"—they had been screams before. Then even the whispers ceased, the beaks could not be opened, and slowly, slowly they starved.

And those are the feathers—feathers that have been got in that way—which the poor women whose hearts the little demon has frozen, wear in their hats. In those hats they go out to concerts, and hear songs that are all of love and tenderness, and music that seems to have been made by the angels in heaven; in those hats they go to meetings that are held, perhaps, for some good and just thing—to save people from being killed, or children from being starved—some of them may even speak at such meetings—and in those hats, those very hats; in those hats, too, they go to church, they kneel down in them, and they pray—yes, *pray*.

Oh, it is wonderful—wonderful! In Africa, where the people believe in witchcraft, one man will throw a spell upon another man that he hates, so that wherever that man goes and whatever he does, he always sees his face, his enemy's face. There it is, always before him, and, at last, he gets so tired of seeing it that he dies, or even kills himself. Of course, he does not *really* see the face, and his enemy does not *really* cast a spell upon him, because there is no such thing as witchcraft, *really*; it is all superstition, as I think you know. But as the one man *thinks* he sees the face, and the other man *thinks* he is casting a spell upon him, and making him see it, it comes to very nearly—if not quite—the same thing as if it were real, especially as the one man does *really* die. Ah, if those hats could cast a spell (not quite the same one as that, but something like it), if, wherever the women who wore them went—whether it was to concerts where they heard beautiful music, or to meetings where good things were talked about, or to church where they kneeled down and prayed—they always saw a picture of a nest, with young birds in it, starving—slowly starving! if it was always there, always before them—that pitiful picture—and if the voices came, too—the screams, and then the whispers—"Feed us! feed us!" then, I think, they would take off those hats, and they would not wear them any more. They need not die or kill themselves, they would only have to take off those hats.

And they will do that now, because you and every little child in the world will have asked them to. Yes, they will do it now. They will take off those hats—those hats of starvation and murder, of terrible and shameful cruelty—they will leave off wearing them, they will never put them on, again. Those plumes called "ospreys," that one sees everywhere—in streets and in shop-windows, at concerts, at meetings, and in churches—that bend above fine sentiments, that wave over charities and goodnesses, and tremble, softly, in the breath that prayers are made of—they will tear them out of their hats and out of their hair—yes, and out of their hearts too. They will hate them, they will loathe them, and when they say, next time, in church, upon their knees, "Give us this day our daily bread," they will try not to remember them, or only to think that they are unfashionable.

Oh, make them unfashionable! for you have not yet, you have not said "promise" yet. Oh, then, at once, at once! Break the spell of the demon, that spell that is so real and so cruel, that spell that kills the soul. Thaw the poor frozen heart, thaw it with your own warm one, with your lips, with your soft hands and arms. Thaw it with the tears in your eyes, as they look up, thaw it with the words that you say,

"Mother, do not kill parents, and make children starve! Mother, do not wear 'ospreys!' Oh, mother, promise, promise!"

So, now, we have saved the White Egrets, as well as all those other birds that I have been telling you of, and that your mother has promised about. But does that save all the beautiful birds in the world? Oh no, for there are ever so many more than I have been able to say anything about, in a little book like this, more—oh, a great many more—than all the Birds of Paradise, and all the Humming-birds, and all the other ones in the other chapters—for, you know, there are not many—put together. And though the Humming-birds and the Birds of Paradise and the White Egrets and the others are, now, quite safe, yet, if your mother does not promise about the rest, people will go on killing them, till there are no more of them left in the world. Think what that would mean! Why, besides hundreds and hundreds of beautiful foreign birds, it would mean all the kingfishers—the star-birds (for there has been no promise about them)—and all the chaffinches and bullfinches and goldfinches and greenfinches—yes, and all the little robin-redbreasts too—being shot and shot, killed and killed, till there were no more of them left, either in England or anywhere else. For, of course, when all the beautiful foreign birds were gone, then the frozen-hearted women would begin to wear our own little birds, here at home, in their hats. You would hear one lady say to another: "I wanted to have a redbreast tippet this winter, but, my *dear* they are so expensive. You see, hundreds go to one, because there's only the breast, so I'm afraid I must fall back on greenfinch. They're less, of course; you see, there's a greater surface, and they're not quite so rare. But I *did* so want redbreast!" And, then, the other lady would say: "Well, I think I should manage it if I were you, dear, for, you know, they say there'll soon be no more real redbreast—only imitation. So it's best to get one, whilst there's time." And you may be sure that it would be managed somehow—things like that always are.

Well, then, but what is to be done? Do you think your mother would make a promise about all the birds? I think she would if *you* were to ask her. But then, perhaps, she might think it a *little* hard not to wear any feathers—just at first, at any rate—although flowers and all sorts of other things look ever so much nicer in hats. Oh, but wait. Are there *no* feathers that can be worn in hats without its doing any harm at all—without any bird being killed to get them? Why, yes, of course there are—and the very handsomest of them all—ostrich-feathers. Ostriches are kept on farms, and twice a year, their beautiful white and black feathers are clipped and sent to the market. So, as they are not killed, but kept alive and fed and taken care of, and have a very good time of it—as I can tell you that they do, for I have lived on an ostrich-farm—I do not see any reason why one should not wear their feathers—if one wants to. And how beautiful their feathers are! I think, myself, that they are the only feathers that really look nice in a hat—at any rate they are the only ones that ever looked nice in a portrait. A portrait of a lady in a beautiful, broad-brimmed hat, with beautiful, broad, soft ostrich-feathers curling all round it, looks lovely; but a portrait of a lady in a stiff little pork-pie sort of thing, with a lot of heads and wings and tails, sticking bolt upright in it, looks *horrid*. People, you know, always look like their portraits, as long as their portraits are good ones—and, of course, we are not talking about bad portraits. So I think that any *sensible* woman, even though her heart were frozen and she were determined to wear feathers, would only wear ostrich-feathers. Of course, no woman whose heart the wicked little demon had *not* frozen would ever wear any other kind.

But there are not going to be frozen-hearted women in the world any more, now, because their little children will soon have thawed all their hearts, and the Goddess of pity is just beginning to wake up again. So now, ask your dear, dear mother to make just one more promise, just one more which will be better than all the others she has made. Of course she could not be expected to make it quite at first, but now, after all that you have told her, I think she will. Just go to her and throw your arms round her neck, and whisper: "Mother, promise not to wear *any* feathers, except the beautiful ostrich-feathers that you look so *lovely* in." As soon as she has promised, then all the beautiful birds in the world (and that means all the birds, for all birds are beautiful) will be saved, and it is you and the other little children who will have saved them. So, of course, you must keep on saying "Promise" till she does.

**END PIECE**

Lector House believes that a society develops through a two-fold approach of continuous learning and adaptation, which is derived from the study of classic literary works spread across the historic timeline of literature records. Therefore, we aim at reviving, repairing and redeveloping all those inaccessible or damaged but historically as well as culturally important literature across subjects so that the future generations may have an opportunity to study and learn from past works to embark upon a journey of creating a better future.

This book is a result of an effort made by Lector House towards making a contribution to the preservation and repair of original ancient works which might hold historical significance to the approach of continuous learning across subjects.

**HAPPY READING & LEARNING!**

**LECTOR HOUSE LLP**
**E-MAIL:** lectorpublishing@gmail.com